Mr. Michael's Music Maker Manual

A Parents' Guide To Growing Creative Children

MICHAEL HEMSWORTH

Copyright © 2025 by Michael Hemsworth.

All rights reserved. No part of this book may be used or reproduced in any form whatsoever without written permission except in the case of brief quotations in critical articles or reviews.

Printed in the United States of America.

For more information, or to book an event, contact :
michael@newsongsmusic.com
http://www.newsongsmusic..com/manual

Book design by Michael Hemsworth
Cover design by Michael Hemsworth

ISBN - Paperback: 978-1-967557-01-1

First Edition: April 2025

CONTENTS

DEDICATION 5

CHAPTER ONE 7
In Defense of Creativity

CHAPTER TWO 20
A Place to Grow

CHAPTER THREE 28
The Garden of the Mind

CHAPTER FOUR 39
Cultivating Aptitude

CHAPTER FIVE 51
Strong Roots

CHAPTER SIX 61
Growth and Opportunity

CHAPTER SEVEN 75
The Learning Cycle

CHAPTER EIGHT 88
Staying Motivated

CHAPTER NINE 105
Sorting Out the Library

CHAPTER TEN Conclusion	**123**
APPENDIX Questions & Answers	**129**
EPILOGUE	**154**
ABOUT THE AUTHOR	**156**

DEDICATION

This work is dedicated first to my dad. I lost him way too soon when I was 19 years old, and I didn't realize it at the time when I was growing up, but my dad was a creative soul. He left space in his heart for the messy, dreamy work of leaving a unique and positive imprint on the world.

My dad made slideshows in the 70s, and by the 90s made videos to promote very small non profits and other organizations. He was never very mainstream, he always worked on the fringes where no one else was. He never made lots of money, he dabbled in lots of side projects, he said "yes" to try things even if it was not always logical. He got into some crazy predicaments, but then he had great stories to tell.

I grew up wanting to be creative, but I did not realize I wanted to be like him. I wanted to be a ventriloquist for a while (I know, not normal right), a Shakespearean actor (because who would want to be a REGULAR actor), or a detective like "Encyclopedia Brown" (maybe slightly more normal), and was involved with music, dance and theater as a teen. I did not realize at the time how special it was for all of these dreams or obsessions to be accepted as normal. Only in retrospect did I see that the bond I shared with my dad--the creative spark that has to be protected and nurtured or else it will get snuffed out. Both of my parents protected that for me, but my dad truly modeled it for himself.

This work is also dedicated to my wife, who has filled that same space in the second half of my life. She is a true "yes" woman for whom nothing is impossible. Despite health conditions that would stop most people, she continually finds new veins to do creative work, and she has been my role model in raising our own creative kids. I could say much more about her, but hopefully you meet her yourself someday and you will understand exactly what I mean when I talk about a person who has kept their creative spark alive.

I believe that creativity is one of the keys to happiness, like Chase Jarvis says, "Creativity is a life amplifier. It's as fundamental to our well-being as physical fitness, proper nutrition, and mindfulness."

Thank you to the people in my life that had the courage to make magic by expressing themselves in the world, no matter what the world gave back to them.

CHAPTER ONE

In Defense of Creativity

"The things that made you weird as a kid make you great as an adult—but only if you pay attention to them." – James Victore

First of all, thank you for taking the time to read this. I started this short book after 20+ years of teaching music and running my own community music school, NewSongs, to support and encourage parents and families to successfully help children in their lives become more creative, particularly by being more musical. Ken Robinson's TED Talk on creativity in education, one of the most viewed of all times, proclaims that "Creativity is as important as literacy, and we should treat it with the same status." I appreciate the fact that you want this too and that we can share this mission together.

Music, along with many other creative disciplines, empowers the user to remember that they have a unique power or voice in the world. There is something you can bring into the world that no one else can. Being creative takes a lot of courage. Elizabeth Gilbert, author of "Eat Pray Love" describes it as "Big Magic". This magic is the true gift we can give our children, hidden into the daily routines of going to music lessons, finishing 15 minutes of daily practice, and victoriously surviving your first piano recital.

In a world where distractions compete for our children's attention at every turn, making music offers something increasingly rare—genuine connection. Instead of just another activity to shuffle between soccer practice and homework, when children complete the full cycle of musical learning, they discover a powerful way to connect with themselves and others that satisfies a fundamental human need to relate and belong.

Music that fails to forge connections often leads nowhere but frustration. I've watched countless students walk away from music lessons because they couldn't see how the notes on the page connected to their lives. But I've also witnessed the magic that happens when those connections click into place.

Music connects us to each other in tangible ways. When my students play in an orchestra, they're not just learning an instrument—they're learning to listen, to adjust, to contribute to something larger than themselves. When they play duets, something remarkable happens in the mirror neurons of the brain as they synchronize and respond to another person in real time. I've seen shy children transform during these collaborative moments, finding their place in a musical conversation.

I have childhood memories involving singing with my grandmother—songs nobody else seems to know anymore. My grandmother lived states away and I did not spend a lot of time with her, but that shared musical experience created bonds that transcended age and time. The same thing happens when families sing together at home or when teenagers belt out lyrics together at karaoke. These aren't just fun activities; they're relationship builders.

There are certainly academic connections as well. My focus will be mostly the social and emotional connections that music makes, but the academic and developmental benefits are significant as well. Amongst many other benefits, musicians recognize patterns and connections in the world around us with a unique ability to spot relationships that others miss. For instance, they might notice how a pop song on the radio borrows chord progressions from a classical piece written centuries ago (yes, Phil Collins' "Groovy Kind of Love" and Clementi's Sonatina in F are connected with a shared melody, just like Bach's Minuet in G and "A Lover's Concerto" by The Toys).

My goal as a teacher is to cultivate wonder in a world that often rushes to explanations before questions are even asked. I love Ted Lasso's wisdom from the television series by the same name: "Be curious, not judgmental." This applies perfectly to raising musical children. Unlike passive media consumption, making music invites continuous exploration. Each time we sit down to play a piece, we can discover something new—a different interpretation, a deeper feeling, a technical breakthrough. The recording always sounds the same, but our musical experiences evolve constantly, fostering a growth mindset that serves children in every area of life.

Perhaps most importantly, music brings joy. As we navigate the mental health challenges facing children growing up in this digital age, making music offers a powerful antidote to isolation and comparison. When we create environments where "sharing" music replaces "winning" or even "succeeding" at music, I've seen genuine smiles light up not just the performers' faces but everyone around them.

I've written this book to help you create spaces where children feel free to sing, free to dance, free to participate in music without fear of judgment. That is when true learning and creative development can occur. It is not because they'll all become professional musicians (though some might), but because of the connections they make through music will enrich their lives immeasurably.

The garden of creativity in a child needs cultivation. Let's tend it together.

Good, But Not Good Enough
(Why We Give Up)

Most people will not argue to me that music education lacks value. Many people, however, will conveniently forget to put the time and energy into making music education happen. It is time to figure out a pathway forward and turn our good intentions into real, tangible growth for the children in our lives. How do we overcome these very real issues we face?

- **There is not enough time** (or resources) in the school day for it
- **There is not enough time after school** for lessons between all of the other sports and recreational activities
- **There is not enough time at home** for a parent to encourage practice and learning at home
- **Adults are intimidated** by their own lack of music experience, and
- "The child is **just not interested** at this time"

When I was 20 years old, I started a school. I started NewSongs because I knew my life calling was to teach and cultivate creativity and there was no place for me to work and do that job the way I envisioned it. I started with 50 business cards I printed on Avery cardstock and some neon colored flyers that I put on the bulletin board at the local library (more about my love of libraries later). I offered a "summer camp" in the tiny living room of my shared 800 sq ft duplex and I taught a few kids about piano basics and listened to the Carnival of the Animals. Even as a budding educator, I wanted to give two things to my students- first an immersive love of music, and second, the skills to actively participate in it.

Twenty-two years later, I am still at it. Lots of things I tried worked, and many more failed. Building a school is a lot like any other artistic endeavor, and the most important tool you have to succeed is showing up every single day, believing in yourself (and having a family or support network that believes in you), and never giving up.

Now, NewSongs runs four locations with weekly lessons for more than 1300 students and serves a dozen other schools and community locations, we have a music bus, and more. When I get up in the morning, though I still basically do the same job I did when I taught my debut camp. Whether it is for 2 kids or 2000, I want every student (adults too, but especially children) to have a place, where they can interact with music more deeply, learn to understand and appreciate things that seem unfamiliar or difficult, and develop the confidence to make music themselves.

Music is a good idea, but often it's just not quite good enough to take the time to cultivate.

Cultivate is a carefully chosen word for me.

Throughout this book I will use analogies of a garden and a gardener. I did not use the garden analogy because I am actually good at gardening. I respect my green-thumbed friends very much, but I enjoy the "fruits" of their work more than the work itself.

I may not have the skills to grow, well, anything. But I can only enjoy a garden that SOMEONE has spent time and effort on. I have visited a few great gardens around the world and have marveled at their beauty. In my own yard, I don't have such beauty, but I can't blame the dirt that "it just was not interested in growing." My own lack of time, knowledge and commitment are definitely at play–but I think the stakes are higher when growing our children, than when growing our yards.

There are some rare musical talents in the world, yes. There are some beautiful wildflowers that grow despite adverse conditions too. But I am not ready to leave all the flowers in the world to grow in a select few places any more than I am ready to leave music only in the hands of a few professionals and prodigies. Anyone can grow a tomato plant if they want fresh vegetables in their life, and anyone can participate in music, if they want it in their life too.

Through this book, I will address some of the obstacles that hold our children back from learning and making music. I will explain what musical aptitude is and when and how to nurture it. Then, I will explore the many valid pathways children can take to engage in music. I am not here to sell you a new or groundbreaking method. There are no secret formulas here that will make you a musical master in half the time. In fact, I hope to dispel the myth that there is one "right" way to approach music education.

You Can't Win (And That's the Point)

Music is not a *"winning"* activity.

Children have grown up seeing reality talent competitions, social media influencers and musicians that sell out massive venues, giving the impression that a select few "win" at the game of music. And by comparison? Most others "lose". But there are no losers in music. I am happy for my students that have won music scholarships, performed paid gigs, and made other musical accomplishments. I am just as proud of the work I have done with students that never took their guitar further than their bedroom or only completed two levels of piano books but did not go "all the way". These students have received just as many social, emotional and cognitive benefits as their counterparts that got more social media likes and fans.

I am not against all forms of competition. Before we judge the proverbial "dance mom" or "helicopter parent" stereotypes, my wife and I took one of our children on the competitive dance circuit for several years (if you have been there with competitive cheerleading, travel soccer, or anything of the sort you know it's like living in an alternative reality...in fact several reality TV series document the phenomenon). You have to go into a competitive world with your eyes wide open to the benefits and the pitfalls. If you bonded with your child in the shared adventure of trying their best in the competitive arena (and provided you made it clear you loved them just as much if they won or lost) then cherish that adventure. I just ask that we all see competitive arts events as a slice, not the whole pie. Playing soccer with your friends has many social and health benefits without dominating in a competitive league. Dancing in your living room can bring as much joy–or more–than taking the big stage at a national competition. It's not all-or-nothing. It is not about winners and losers. Please never say that just because you will not win on "American Idol" that you are "not a singer".

That brings me to one pet peeve of mine. I have met far too many adults who were told, sometime in their adolescence, that they were not good enough for making music. There are many variations of this statement, but everyone got the message loud and clear. Someone told them to be quieter, find another activity, or to give up hope in their musical journey. I think this kind of elitism has no place in the musical world. Unless you raised your hand to say, "I want to fight to be the best in my musical field and I am willing to be rated and ranked in my effort to rise to the top," it is nobody's business to be judging those around us. We cannot protect our kids from every judgement that will come along, but we need to work hard to counteract the damage from them. If I had a dollar for every person I met that quit music because they were told that they were not talented enough, I would be a rich man. Let's work to change the narrative everyone. Ok, rant over.

Parents, this includes judging your child that "just won't practice." I promise you every child will go through a season where practicing is a struggle. Please do not communicate during hard times that your child is not musical, lazy, bad, untalented or any variation thereof. Don't give away their guitar because they haven't played in the last six months. Don't pull them out of choir and never look back because "we tried that once and it did not work". It is not all-or-nothing, win or lose.

How Did I Get Here? (And Where Do We Go Next?)

Now you know what "ruffles my feathers" so to speak. Let me share just a little bit of where I come from. I am something of a folksy-nerd. I got a degree in classical piano at the age of 18. I was never "cool." Never even tried. I grew up in the 80s with older and more conservative parents so I can hardly name most of the music from the 80s and 90s. I can name thousands of pieces from the 1880s though. I love to name the classical music in the background of commercials, and yet none of my three kids are ever impressed.

I am a middle child. I am a highly visual learner and academically talented–I love the library (I was a teenage volunteer to reshelve books during summer vacation...I told you I was a nerd), I am a good test-taker, and actually have fun writing essays. I mean–I am writing this book now for you, and having a great time doing it. This also meant I was well equipped to succeed in traditional school environments.

I am not anti-technology, but I am also not a gamer, and grew up with a desktop computer in the family room but never my own video game console. I have always loved the arts and I have never been good at sports. I got married young, and my wife would laugh at my attempts to play basketball in my 20s after a lifetime of...well, not playing basketball. We started a family at a young age, which I loved. We were both born to be parents, and the imaginative world of early childhood is very comfortable for me. Mr. Rogers is my lifelong hero (more in the next chapter). I love going to Disneyland (never went as a child so my mind was blown as a young parent going for the first time). I am hopelessly optimistic.

I share these things because we all have a viewpoint. We all have a life experience. Many parents I talk to never had a parent or grandparent that sang to them. I remember songs that no one else seems to know anymore. That became part of the background that cultivated my own musical development. But if you grew up listening to ACDC or country western with someone in your life, that is no better or no worse. My hope is to encourage you to recognize your own musical history, as much or as little as it was, and authentically use that. It's OK to drum along to "Smoke on the Water" with your toddler just as much as it is to play

Mozart next to their crib.

A fellow parent that I work with recounts her experience this way: "Growing up, at the dinner table with six children we would love to talk until inevitably someone would burst out singing and make us all want to join in. It would usually be Cher, Neil Diamond, Tina Turner, Eric Clapton, Rod Steward... many amazing artists. I consider that the soundtrack to my life. One of the last memories I have of my mother was when she ordered my siblings and I to get into her new car... Cher started playing on the car radio and we were instructed to sing "it's in his kiss" as loud as we possibly could. She passed away two weeks later at the young age of 39. Throughout the years, music was my therapy. As a mom, music is my kid's therapy. We dance on a bad day off and celebrate a good day with dance! None of us ever became professional musicians, but we were certainly actively engaged with music. None of us were ever too shy or scared to sing at school and take a singing class or dance all of a sudden to our favorite song in the mall! Music provided us with confidence, with a way to process our feelings, and connect with others. Music is surely magical!"

When we give up on making music "in real life", we miss out on helping our kids connect with themselves, connect with others, develop their growing brains and most of all miss out on the joy of making music. Despite the challenges though, making music is attainable and accessible for all of us. Let's get started together.

Key Takeaways

- Music and creative education aren't easy, but they are vital. The challenge is part of the magic.

- Just like a garden, music grows through both natural talent and careful tending. When we recognize and nurture these traits in our children, we give them room to bloom.

- There is no singular "right way" to approach music education. The journey matters more than the destination.

What's Next

Creativity isn't just a nice-to-have—it's essential. It's what gives kids the confidence to explore, to make mistakes, and to find their own voice in the world. In the first chapter, we looked at why creativity matters, especially in music, and how easily it gets lost when we focus too much on perfection. But creativity doesn't grow in a vacuum—it needs a place to take root. That's where the next chapter comes in. Just like Mr. Rogers' "Neighborhood of Make-Believe" gave kids a safe space to explore big ideas, we need to create environments where kids feel free to make and believe. Because when children know they can create without judgment, they don't just learn music—they learn resilience, curiosity, and joy.

CHAPTER TWO

A Place to Grow

"Imagining something may be the first step in making it happen, but it takes the real-time work of growing to turn it into reality." –Fred Rogers

The Neighborhood of Make Believe.

My personal hero is Fred Rogers, or "Mr Rogers" of "Mr Rogers' Neighborhood". I don't have a lot of memories of watching Mr Rogers as a child in the 80s. My mother really didn't like television so it was limited, but my dad did like TV, so we always had Friday nights free for watching. I did have a childhood phase where I wanted to be a puppeteer (like the puppets in the neighborhood, mostly voiced by Mr Rogers himself). Now as an adult, I appreciate the sincere way he held his own child-likeness open and treated children as equals. I don't believe in treating children like miniature adults, but I do believe in treating them with the same inherent dignity and value.

"Mr Roger's Neighborhood" had "The Neighborhood of Make Believe". The Neighborhood of Make-Believe served as a space where children could explore various situations and emotions through storytelling and character interactions, facilitating learning and emotional growth. It was a distinct place, because only "real" things would happen in the real world of the show, and imaginary things like Daniel Tiger and the other puppet characters were found in the land of Make Believe. Guest characters like Big Bird from Sesame Street could only visit the neighborhood of Make Believe (unless they were willing to show that there was a real person under the costume).

I hope this book is a guide creating a "Neighborhood of Make Believe" for you and your child today. A safe, imaginative and creative space is critical for emotional awareness and self confidence, and making music can provide that space for a developing child. Being a music maker is a very personal and introspective thing, but it is also called a neighborhood because of the human connections created through music (and the arts in general). These connections are vital to growing a healthy and well-rounded small human.

Make. Believe

It is called Make Believe because we **make it**. I believe humans are creative beings.

I have heard hundreds of traumatic stories from people who now believe they are "not creative" or "not musical". My mother (the one who doesn't like TV) played the piano as a child, but entered a competition at one point, badly forgot part of her solo on stage, and has felt like she could not successfully enjoy playing music ever since. Fortunately for me, she still got a piano into the house when I was about 11 years old and started my journey for me, but she would rarely touch it herself.

When we lose the ability to "make" things we have lost a fundamental power that everyone deserves to have. It is the confidence that we don't just have to FIND the answer to unsolved problems, we can CREATE the solution. (More about innovation and the practical impacts of creativity for 21st century citizens later on.)

Second, it is "make BELIEVE" because this call to be musical and artistic gives us, and our children, a grounded self-confidence or anchor as they grow. They can believe in themselves. This has nothing to do with religious beliefs. Believing in SOMETHING is one of the keys to lifelong happiness and satisfaction, so you may as well believe in yourself and the things that you are able to make.

Making music could mean composing your own song on the piano to express your feelings. It could be singing karaoke with friends on a Friday night. It could be the ability to march and dance to the beat around the house when the music comes on. I am going to talk a lot about music education and instruction. Just like math education is not just for those who will grow up to be mathematicians and engineers, and learning to read is not just for professional writers, music education is about the tools to PARTICIPATE in music. It is about empowering people to hear music and feel like they can engage with it actively instead of passively.

Being a maker is about being involved.

The opposite of believing in yourself as a maker is not being "unmusical". It is being a consumer without the power to be a producer. Making music is not a gift for a select few, it is a privilege for all of us, if we have the confidence to do it.

What is a "Creator"?

We all know the unfortunate trend where our kindergarten students, when asked "What do you want to be when you grow up?" reply not with astronaut or teacher but with "content creator." I cringe at the thought of my child as a professional game streamer or toy unboxer on YouTube too.

As we will look at later, I believe that music and art fall into several broad categories, including popular music that makes money, folk music that is part of a shared cultural experience and art or classical music that stretches the boundaries and tries to present specific ideas. I know that of course is a huge overgeneralization, but stay with me. I see many children today only connect "creators" with commercial success or popularity.

I mean, I am guilty too. I have watched more reality TV this year than I have watched critically acclaimed art films. I have been too tired to go out for a cultural event when I could stay in and shop online. Being "too commercialized" is hard to avoid.

But here is my cautionary tale. We have to protect our

children from the perception that music is only for professionals, or paid (hopefully highly-paid) people. We need more places where "everyone sings in the choir" to normalize active music making for everyone, as opposed to "we searched the country and ONE talented person gets to be the winning singer of American Idol".

The message is all around that making things is only for the best and the brightest and if you can't be the best at something, go try something else. At our music school, I get messages every week that people are stopping music lessons because they are not playing enough at home and so they are "no longer interested" (which I usually interpret to mean the parent, child, or both have lost the belief that they can make music successfully). Not every student will spend ten years studying music. Too many students get zero years nowadays. I think every student should have at least years (meaning, not three months and quitting) of active music education. This could be in school, in lessons, or with family at home.

Why be a creator? There are many models that a creator doesn't have to work, enjoys money and fame and things appear to always be easy and fun. Real creatives know that it is great work leading to great rewards. Elizabeth Gilbert ("Eat Pray Love") talks about the creative life as something you feel you MUST do. Professional creatives are a special bunch of people with a special calling. Creators looking for easy money by being viral on the internet are not the creatives I am hoping to grow, because art for the sake of commercial success is only one small piece of the artistic pie.

"Resilience, in many ways, is our ability to experience a wide range of emotions and still feel like ourselves. Resilience helps us bounce back from the stress, failure, mistakes, and adversity in our lives. Resilience allows for the emergence of happiness." - Dr Becky Kennedy "Good Inside"

The Seed

Imagine being a tiny seed. There are hundreds, maybe thousands of things you may grow up to be...

Some trees will take a hundred years to finish growing. Other flowers and even weeds can sprout up overnight. Some things sound dangerous. Some are rare and stand out, and others are incredibly common and you are safe blending in.

The internet has changed things. There are ranking boards, and you can tell exactly how popular every plant is going to be.

What are you hoping to grow up to be?

This is the challenge of being a child. What pathways are worth the effort and pain? Is the most popular choice the right one?

Just as the flower seed in Eric Carle's "The Tiny Seed" and the seed of a tree in "Because of an Acorn" by Schaefer &

Schaefer, keeping authentic, personal creativity alive comes with opposition. These are things I have heard many times about kids and teens that are deeply involved in music or other arts:

- "Will you really make it?"

- "Why would you choose to be so different?"

- "It seems dangerous, here are safer options out there"

Opposition comes from both these outside voices and internal fears. Self-doubt is always present, blocking the creative spirit. But the futures that we are the most afraid to pursue, may be the most important ones.

Key Takeaways

- Creativity is about empowering children to believe they can create.

- Comparison is a roadblock to a child's personal creative journey.

- Creativity builds confidence and a sense of ownership to choose your destiny/ destination.

What's Next

Creating space for creativity isn't just about providing opportunities—it's about building an environment where children feel safe to explore, experiment, and sometimes fail without fear. In the last chapter, we looked at how imagination and self-expression are vital for confidence, and how a "Neighborhood of Make-Believe" can give kids the freedom to make and believe in themselves. But creativity needs more than space—it needs *nourishment*. Just like a garden, the mind requires careful tending, *patience*, and the right conditions to *grow*. In the next chapter, we'll dig into what it means to cultivate creativity in children—not as rigid "carpenters" trying to build a perfect product, but as gardeners, allowing each child to flourish in their own way, at their own pace.

CHAPTER THREE

The Garden of the Mind

"Our job as parents is not to make a particular kind of child. Instead, our job is to provide a protected space of love, safety, and stability in which children of many unpredictable kinds can flourish." Allison Gopnik, "The Gardener and the Carpenter"

The Parent as the Generous Gardener

I first encountered contrasting parenting styles analogous to a gardener and a carpenter in "The Anxious Generation" by Jonathan Haidt.

My mother was a carpenter. She was and is a loving parent and sincerely wanted good for her children. She searched for as long as I can remember for the "best" blueprints and plans to produce good children. She read all the parenting books, took the classes, and constantly self-criticized over her own parenting "failures". Carpenters, in that sense, can be graded or judged by how closely their final product matched the blueprint. And my siblings and I were wildly different…so that must mean something fell short of the master plan. The carpenter is generally marked by more rules and expectations.

My father was more of a gardener, though probably a somewhat carefree one. He too was a loving parent, who often stated that when the Bible said "raise up a child in the way he should go" that is meant the way HE should go (not the way EVERYONE should go, but that the pathway for each person was individual). He was, however, more likely to throw some seeds on the ground and "hope for the best". The gardener usually leaves some "wide open space" for growth.

My mother was not unloving—just the opposite. She put in tons of effort as a parent (remember all the parenting books she read?) and showed plenty of unconditional love and affection. Carpenter parents can often be extremely attentive and loving, and almost always have good intentions.

I believe the carpenter model is ultimately an exercise in futility for most. Carpenters build with dead wood and gardeners work with living plans. As long as our children are living spirits they cannot be molded, bent or broken into a consistent shape...at least without also getting damaged along the way.

I also believe that many of us as parents come to a point of giving up on our "gardens". To get literal here, I have given up on the plants in my yard (I don't think it's fair to have ever called it a "garden"). If it got really bad, I would probably have to stage a yard intervention on myself, but for now there are two hydrangeas outside by door, one is much more alive than the other (I think maybe it has to do with the difference in shade?) and neither is as healthy or full as it could be. But I feel like "I tried" and that "it's good enough" so there they stay.

As parents it is pretty easy to feel the same way about our children as they grow. Because no matter how many books you have read or strategies you have tried, the results of your own child are going to be inconsistent. So are we actually even doing it right?

So it's possible with the right plans and skills I could build a perfect fence. It's not possible to grow a perfect garden where the squash are all the right shape and size, the correct numbers of strawberries and tomatoes grow, and the weeds eventually all go away.

Our kids are not wildflowers either. We don't just feed and clothe them and hope it all works out in the end (and yes, some of us as adults can say that is exactly how they were raised, and it is true you survived but do you really think it was actually the ideal scenario?)

We need a vision for what our children can be. As they grow, they get to contribute to the vision as well.

Our oldest child is, in many ways, a typical oldest child. She got very comfortable hanging out with adults and developed a grown up vocabulary quickly, she (mostly) behaved as expected, especially in public, and participated in a variety of activities from gymnastics to arts and crafts camps and more. (We didn't do as well on the kids' sports until our second and third. So, sorry Honey, for the lack of sports knowledge).

Our second child is a boy, now the middle child, just like I was as the middle son in my own family. But he could not have been more different from me, or from his older sister. My wife became the ultimate gardener to help him find his own way in the world. Amid many, many things that make my son unique, he has auditory processing disorder. This means that some sounds tend to get scrambled from brain to ears, so phonics was tough, and strings of verbal directions were hard because his brain needed more time to sort out what he was hearing.

It's easy as a parent to feel like you are failing. My son spoke much later than my daughter, and even proactive steps like speech therapy were not paying off. We tried testing his hearing, and wondered about ADHD, but it was like a puzzle. My wife finally cracked the code when she began researching auditory processing disorder, and subsequently sought therapies that targeted APD for him. He could not follow in his sister's footsteps into the "garden". He could memorize what words looked like but struggled to sound them out. Instead of getting stuck on the problem, we found another way in, another gate into the garden. That included academic therapies, but also included karate, where visual cues always accompanied verbal cues so he could put them together, and even things like phonics games online. My daughter loved showing off her progress as she learned, but my son was much more introverted and wanted to practice privately and not always have someone watching him or working with him.

I am not suggesting we did everything correctly, but I do want to demonstrate that we took very different approaches with our children. Often with music, we take one approach and give up or, worse, blame the child for just not trying hard enough. Instead as parents and teachers, we need more tools to create an environment where all kids can grow.

When it comes to growing a creative child, the process is a lot like growing a garden. New gardens may not produce much the first year, but that should not be a reason to stop trying. A good gardener works to create the healthiest soil possible, adding fertilizer and removing weeds, encouraging, not forcing, things to grow. How exactly to nourish the soil may require some trial and error. Additionally, growing creativity and growing plants can require moderation at times. You can water a plant too much, and you can inundate a student with too many expectations and requirements as well. Plants need water and artists and musicians need practice. But hopefully it is OK to have seasons where kids practice more or less time each day. Remember that seasons change. And remember that is you only grow tomatoes (the equivalent of only using one book, one style of music, or one approach) you could miss out on discovering other types of plants, or talents, that may grow more easily or joyfully.

Here is the challenge. Some of the flowers will die. Some of the tomatoes will be inedible. It won't all work. But instead of giving up and letting whatever wild plants do what they want, I hope to be willing to try some things again, or give up on others in order to try again with something new.

To extend the analogy of the garden, we all have some "nature" to our musical aptitudes along with some "nurture" to the skills we grow. One person's garden could be naturally suited to easily grow tomatoes while another could bloom easily with wildflowers (while growing tomatoes may take extra time and attention before they start producing to their full potential).

In addition to some things growing more easily from one garden to another, each gardener has preferences for how they want to enjoy their garden. At the end of the day, it doesn't matter if you can easily grow giant zucchini, if it's the one vegetable you refuse to eat.

So a healthy musical mind, or "garden", will always allow one to remember and create/recreate melodies, feel, move or play to the beat, and connect with music in an expressive way. Beyond that, the rock and roll section of your garden could be overflowing with blooms or the orchestral rows could be growing a bumper crop.

'Parent' is not actually a verb, not a form of work, and it isn't and shouldn't be directed toward the goal of sculpting a child into a particular kind of adult." Allison Gopnik

Getting into the Garden
(Gateways to Creativity)

Here is the issue: imagine your garden is fenced in, and when you enter the gate you are faced with your least favorite plants, or the plants that are going to take the most work to survive. If that was me, I would turn right around, shut the gate and leave that garden behind, claiming that I "am just not the gardening type". Starting music lessons can feel like this.

What if instead, you walked into your garden and were met with the healthiest and most pleasing plants first? I would want to come back every day, gradually working more and more in my whole garden, even the parts that need more work, until I became a "real gardener". This can also be a more inviting way to get started learning to play a musical instrument.

The reality is, there is no need to create fences or gates around our gardens. There is not one "right" place to start. You can walk into any part of the garden that appeals to you and begin to explore.

What are the major "starting places"? When it comes to learning to make music, typically one of major senses or learning styles: eyes (visual), ears (auditory) or touch and feel (kinesthetic). One of the most powerful things about studying music is the blending of these three areas, creating a very "sticky" experience for the brain (do you ever wonder why you can recall songs you sang along to 30 years ago when you can't remember what you ate for lunch yesterday?). We all have dominant strengths and weaknesses in these areas.

For instance, I am a highly visual learner. When I started an app-based journey to learn Italian as an adult, I could read Italian much more easily than I could hear and interpret it. The same was true of learning the piano as a preteen. I love sheet music. Printed music scores are like security blankets to me. They make sense to me.

This left me with other comparative weaknesses. Memorizing music was a struggle (weaker "muscle memory"), and playing music "by ear" took literally decades to not be terrifying, and I am still only moderately skilled in this area.

Imagine if I entered through the "garden gate" of having someone play me a song and ask me to recreate it by ear? It would have been like walking in and seeing a row of sickly looking carrots (my least favorite vegetable–sorry carrot lovers). I would probably walk right back out again.

Similarly, as a teacher in my first decade, I would struggle with students that just could not click with a traditional music reading method book. We would work for three or four weeks on a page that took other students 15 minutes to understand. Was this child not trying? Not musically talented? I knew these things were not true.

So over time I learned to pivot. I learned much more about "rote songs" that could be learned by memorization, and how many skills a young piano player could develop learning to perform a song without any sheet music in front of them. I became willing to put away the book and allow the student in front of me to enter the "garden" from a different perspective, where things grew more easily and enjoyably. They could play songs, even complex songs, using ear and feel based knowledge without ever having to look at any printed music.

Staying in The Garden

Did I eventually want them to explore more of the garden? Absolutely. Reading sheet music opens up opportunities for a musician that others do not get. The ability to write down one's own music (while less critical today thanks to the use of technological tools) is valuable. All the information available from videos and podcasts and the ability to record your own thoughts with voice memos, has not made reading and writing obsolete. The more tools in your tool belt, or for the sake of the extended metaphor, the more gardening tools in your shed, the more well-rounded the mind becomes.

I have worked with some students who started by playing their favorite rock riffs, and then used that passion to springboard into jazz theory, music reading skills, and sometimes, even into a classical music degree. This is the way I hope it works: find an opening into the musical world that works for you and then keep exploring to your heart's content

I have worked with many more students that met resistance "at the gate". They were bored or frustrated on their first approach and they gave up and never looked back. Lets help children find the joy in music first, and then keep in mind that they can continue to grow in new ways. As a child I grew to like broccoli first, but I didn't stop there. Eventually I liked all the vegetables. Carrots came last. I still eat them, but they are not my favorite. What if I was forced to like carrots before I could try any other vegetables? I may have grown up to only eat hamburgers....

Key Takeaways

- We can't control exactly how our children will express their creativity, but we can create an environment that allows them to flourish.

- Like plants, creative and musical skills grow differently for each child—some thrive easily, while others take patience and coaxing. Start with what grows naturally.

- Instead of forcing a rigid outcome, we should embrace the possibility of trying things a different way.

What's Next

If creativity is a garden, then musical ability is one of its most fascinating plants—one that needs both patience and the right conditions to flourish. In the last chapter, we explored how children thrive when we nurture their individuality instead of trying to mold them into a predetermined shape. But what exactly are we growing? And how do we ensure that the soil is rich enough for deep musical roots to take hold? That's where the idea of *cultivating aptitude* comes in. Just as language is absorbed long before a child learns to read, musical understanding begins long before formal lessons ever start. In the next chapter, we'll explore how early exposure, exploration, and playful engagement set the foundation for lifelong musicianship—because a child's musical future isn't determined by talent alone, but by the environment we create around them.

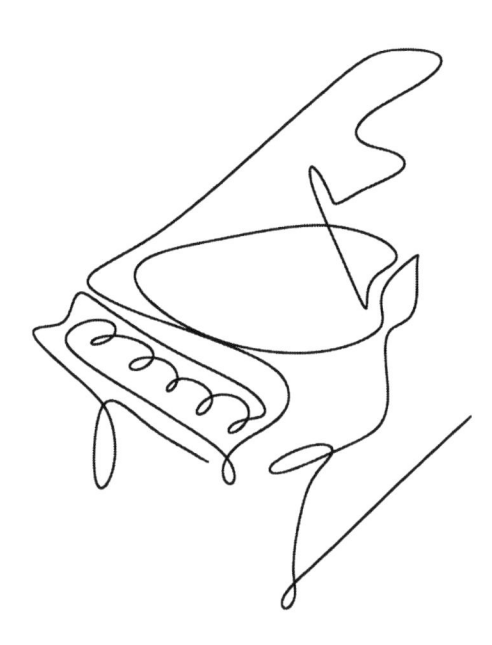

CHAPTER FOUR

Cultivating Aptitude

Are You Ready For It?

There are bits of practical advice out in the world about when children are "ready" for music lessons. It is both well meaning and sometimes incomplete.

Let's draw a parallel to spelling. It is a lot easier (and quicker) to teach a third grader how to spell "thunder" and "bicycle". But that does not mean that as a parent or as a teacher I just wait until third grade to begin teaching spelling. For an adult who has been extending my "streak" on Duolingo to learn Italian, I realize that remembering the vocabulary for garden and music is more efficient at my age than as a preschooler. But was I not "ready" to learn Italian until now? No, of course not, my learning is just different at different developmental ages. The native mastery that a preschooler will gain when immersed in the Italian language will surpass whatever proficiency I manage to gain as an adult.

Most of us have been told as parents how critical reading to our babies, toddlers and preschoolers is, even though they are not "ready" to read by themselves yet. Music is very much the same. The nurturing and cultivating done to give students a lifetime of musical aptitude is very different from the skill-building training provided to older children. We should "wait" to give students developmentally appropriate tasks when they are learning a musical instrument. But don't wait to be purposefully engaged in music and give children the richest "soil" they can for the rest of their lives.

Research by Edwin Gordon, author of the Music Learning Theory, indicates that in early childhood (starting at birth and capping somewhere around the age of 7) a child's brain is actually building all of the musical potential they will have for a lifetime. After that age, a person takes the "soil" of the mind and studies to USE that musical capacity to its full potential. This may be why the concept of "perfect pitch", which is largely elusive and makes college music majors jealous of others that have it, seems to develop best in children that grow up around a language with a basis in pitch. These children have been exposed to listening carefully to distinguish between pitches daily since birth, and it is much harder to develop that sort of critical listening later in life.

Exploration → Integration → Mastery

Every musical journey begins with curiosity and play. Young musicians explore sounds, rhythms, and movement long before they understand them—just as children babble before speaking in full sentences. This stage is about engagement and discovery—clapping along to a song, experimenting with different notes, or recognizing familiar melodies. There is no pressure to "get it right"; the goal is to develop a love for music and build comfort with sound.

As students grow, they begin to connect the dots between what they hear, see, and play. Technique, notation, and listening all merge—students recognize patterns in written music, understand how melodies fit into chord structures, and notice how small adjustments improve their playing. This phase strengthens connections, making learning more fluid and intuitive. A student may start by playing a song by ear, then explore how it looks in notation, or improvise with a scale to internalize its structure. The more ways they engage with musical ideas, the more naturally their understanding deepens.

True mastery isn't about perfection—it's about confidence and fluency. A student reaches this stage when music feels like a language they can speak, rather than just a set of rules they imitate. Mastery builds through consistent practice, layered learning, and a balance between structured guidance and personal expression. By this stage, musicians aren't just following instructions—they're making artistic choices, interpreting pieces with their own voice, and applying their skills across various styles. Most importantly, mastery is not a final destination but a lifelong process of growth, refinement, and creative discovery.

At the Beginning of the Road to Mastery (Music Learning Theory)

As children mature, they begin refining their musical

aptitude. According to Music Learning Theory, this process follows a natural sequence:

Listening → Imitation → Audiation → Improvisation → Notation and Reading

Audiation—"inner hearing" or thinking musically—is a crucial step, enabling children to anticipate and understand music internally. Listening, imitation, and internalization are the foundation, continuing throughout life. As children grow, they must experiment and apply their musical ideas in hands-on ways.

At all stages, **access to instruments matters**, but musical guidance should not be overly rigid. Improvisation—creating music using familiar patterns—builds confidence and independence.

A simplified version of this process looks like this:

- A child hears Mary Had a Little Lamb **(Listening)**

- They sing it back **(Imitation)** until they can recall it independently **(Audiation)**

- The song uses just three notes, so they experiment with those notes on an instrument **(Improvisation)**

- Eventually, they learn to read (or write) with sheet music **(Notation and Reading)**

Many children ages 8-12 begin formal lessons without prior musical experiences. They need time to internalize these steps before reading music fluently. If they don't "get it" immediately, don't be discouraged. A child doesn't learn to speak, let alone read or write, in a few weeks or months. The same patience applies to music.

In the next chapter, we'll explore the essential **pillars of musical growth** and how to build them.

Spiraling Growth

Melanie Bowles, author of the *KeyNotes Music Program*, highlights the importance of **cyclical learning**—revisiting key concepts (like rhythm, pitch, and notation) at increasing levels of complexity over time. Instead of expecting students to master a concept in one lesson, cyclical learning allows for gradual internalization, making learning feel natural.

Why This Matters:

1. **Supports Long-Term Retention** – Repeated exposure strengthens neural connections, moving knowledge into long-term memory.

2. **Reduces Learning Anxiety** – Students feel less pressured to "master" a skill in one attempt, fostering a growth mindset.

3. **Encourages Deep Understanding** – Engaging with concepts in multiple ways (singing, playing, listening)

builds broader connections.

4. **Aligns with Natural Development** – Children grasp ideas at different rates; revisiting concepts allows organic progression.

5. **Enhances Musical Creativity** – Repeated engagement in new contexts fosters creative confidence in improvisation, composition, and performance.

=A *spiral curriculum*, based on Jerome Bruner's educational research, reinforces this approach: complex concepts can be introduced early in simple forms, then revisited with increasing depth over time. This method makes learning feel manageable and connected, rather than overwhelming.

Listening
(The First Step)

We have already been establishing the link between our understanding of musical development and language development. I have some encouragement for parents and teachers. First, just like you talk and read directly to your child, you can sing and play for and with them as well. Recorded music is great, and I think we should use even more of it, but please also bring music "IRL" (in real life).

To help your child listen, share your own love of music. If you love to sing to Shania Twain or Beyonce- go for it. Please normalize singing as an activity that all people can participate in. Culturally, I work with many students that have lost the understanding that singing with and for other people is acceptable. Even in places where people do sing in public, such as in church or singing along at a concert, the "normal" people are largely drowned out by the "professionals."

To that end, most of us don't sound like Mariah Carey when we start to belt out "All I want for Christmas is You." It is important to also help students listen to musical material they can really "work with". Consider "Mary Had a Little Lamb." Children proudly play that tune on the piano all the time (at least for me!). It is familiar and recognizable to most people, and it requires only three notes so it is manageable to sing, remember, and "figure out" on an instrument.

Songs like that generally have 3 to 5 notes in them, are like the vocabulary words in the books "Hop on Pop" or "The Cat in the Hat." They are very attainable for a child in their musical development. They are easier to sing with and for children, and useful for future exploration. Think of them as the musical equivalent of Dr. Seuss books. If you ever listened to music by Raffi or similar artists as a child, his songs worked so well because they stuck to a limited note range that fit a young singing voice

Just like it is useful to read your child many types of books, listening to all types of music has value, but just like selecting books that are going to be easy to "decode" as a child learns to read, filling them with simple songs also sets them up with the internal language of music they can use next.

Doing and Explaining

After we listen, we speak. Musically, we help children first by singing.

What are a few other tools for "doing"? Children need to develop a foundation of moving to a steady beat, so they "do" by marching or moving in an organized fashion, or playing simple (even homemade) instruments to a beat. Drum away! Go crazy (sometimes), but also model and encourage children to find and keep the beat.

Other simple things that children can do is to play simple instruments, like piano keys, which can be great because they provide a very literal layout of the sounds from low to high for students to both see and hear.

In music lessons both parents and teachers often focus on "doing." It is important to realize that doing is not the beginning, and it is also not the end of the process. Thorough, well-rounded learning, starts with listening, and it continues on well after the "doing" is done.

Teaching using questions is a powerful tool, and perhaps I will write again about this teaching tool. Asking questions in a music lesson, or during practice at home, helps students master and explain what they have just done. Group classes can be a wonderful venue for students to experience this kind of growth, because they can actually explain what they are doing to their peers in a "real life" context, and in doing so solidify their own learning. For this discussion, I want to keep moving on and encourage parents and teachers to help students grow past the budding stage of doing and on to blossoming into musical independence.

Experimenting

Let's walk through things that a child may have done now.

A cyclical approach in music lessons might look like this:

- A young child hears a variety of rhythm patterns. They also clap short and long patterns in echo to internalize basic rhythm.

- As they continue to learn, they encounter the same rhythms in a simple song they sing.

- Later, they play the rhythms on an instrument, seeing how they translate to different contexts. They may or may not learn to read or write down this rhythm at this time

- Eventually, they use those rhythms in an improvisation or composition, demonstrating mastery in a personal, creative way.

Hopefully you see that this is not an assembly line process of inputs and then output results or activities, but much more like seeds in the ground. They may be growing for a long period of time "beneath the surface" and without many visible signs. If we do not abandon these young seeds, one day they sprout up–sometimes while we least expect it!

Allowing this process to unfold over time, and without literal steps we can allow children to "think musically" and develop musical familiarity and mastery in accordance with their own cognitive development. Students are engaged and music becomes more intuitive and less intimidating.

Musical Independence

Cyclical learning has another important benefit. Students on a straight line journey (learning anything, not just music) have a challenge: most of the time the journey ahead is longer than the journey behind. Benjamin Hardy and Dan Sullivan describe this as "The Gap and The Gain." The Gap is the amount of learning that is still to come. In other words–at my first piano recital, how much farther do I have to go to compare with the more advanced piano players that also perform. The Gain is the learning that has been completed, or the victory of going from not being able to play the piano at all into someone that can perform a song on stage.

As both adults and children, it can be challenging to focus on the gain, and provide ourselves motivation to keep going, as opposed to the gap, which can be an inundating amount of work "still to go." Cyclical learning, with an emphasis on revisiting and building on past concepts, can also help children have practical experiences to remind them of the gain, or how much they have learned.

Independence can mean:

- A student is able to take simple piece of sheet music and "decode" or perform it without teacher guidance

- A student can hear a simple song and figure out the pattern of sounds on their own

- A student can play or improvise their own creative song

- A student can perform a completed piece of music for others.

- A student can begin a new piece of music and begin to ask questions or look for patterns to understand how the song is put together.

Key Takeaways

- Music in early childhood is like language development—exposure matters, and early experiences shape a lifelong relationship with music.

- As children grow, music learning follows a pattern: first, they do, then they *understand,* then they *explain.* Just like learning to talk, read, and master language.

- Early exposure to music helps children experience

stronger feedback loops about their own musical progress

What's Next

Building musical aptitude is a process—one that starts with curiosity and playful exploration before moving into more structured learning. But even the richest soil won't grow strong plants without solid roots. Just like language, music is absorbed through different senses, and every child has a natural way of processing it—through touch, hearing, or sight. Some kids will instinctively tap rhythms on every surface they see, others will hum melodies effortlessly, and some will be drawn to the patterns in written notation. In the next chapter, we'll explore how these three core learning pathways—*touch, ears, and eyes*—form the foundation of a well-rounded musician. By recognizing and nurturing a child's natural strengths while gently expanding their weaker areas, we can help them develop deep, resilient musical roots that will support them for a lifetime.

CHAPTER FIVE

Strong Roots

The Three Pathways - Touch, Ears & Eyes

Music and neuroscience are amazing partners, because musical development affects most major functions in the brain, linking them together and making them stronger. Recognizing this fact, learning music can either be a joyful experience about building on your strengths, or can be a terrible experience about dwelling on your weaknesses.

Musical learning engages three primary sensory pathways—touch, hearing, and sight—each representing a crucial component of comprehensive musicianship:

1. **TOUCH (Technique):** The physical skills needed to make music on an instrument

2. **EARS (Auditory Skills):** The ability to process, remember, and recreate musical sounds

3. **EYES (Reading Skills):** The capacity to understand and interpret written musical notation

Most children naturally gravitate toward one of these learning pathways. By recognizing and supporting a child's dominant learning style while gradually developing the others, parents and teachers can create a more effective and enjoyable musical journey. Let's explore each of these pillars.

TOUCH (Technique)

What I would traditionally call "techniques".are the actual physical skills needed to make music on an instrument, and like with any activity, the better your physical skills are the more free you are to do that activity.

Take typing as an example. My dad was the king of odd jobs, so I did a variety of things to earn money as a teenager. If my dad met someone new, he would be working on a project for them (or roping his kids into doing it) within the first hour. That's how I spent one summer listening to cassette tapes of nurses' testimonies and typing out the notes. I got paid by the tape, so the faster I worked the more lucrative it was for me and I was paying my way to a summer arts camp. So with all of that practice, you can imagine I am pretty fast typing now.

Typing is a physical skill, a technique. You can type something with poor technique, but it takes a lot longer, and eventually you could create problems like carpal tunnel syndrome. Good technique is important.

Also, technique is usually not that "fun". The effortless looking effects of doing something with good technique is a lot of fun, but the process to get there usually is not. It is repetitive and detail oriented and others never see how much hard work you really did.

This is why a lot of music playing apps are appealing. They get right to performing songs and spend little or no time on the technical skills. But just like growing up and never learning how to type properly, eventually this can backfire.

If we compare music to language, technique is like learning to speak.

EARS - Auditory skills

Auditory skills in music are much like learning to understand spoken language—just as children learn to recognize words and phrases before reading or writing, they also develop a sense of musical sound before reading notation. The most obvious auditory skill is playing "by ear," which often brings to mind viral videos of musicians who can hear a song once and instantly play it back. While this kind of extreme skill is impressive, it's not the standard expectation for most students. Playing by ear is not a rare talent reserved for the musically gifted—it's a skill that all children can develop with the right guidance and practice.

Auditory skills are at the heart of how children memorize, perform, and express music naturally. Nearly every child can sing or hum a song they've heard multiple times, even if they've never seen the notes written down. This ability to audiate or "imagine" music internally—to hear a melody in their mind before playing it—helps with everything from learning new pieces to playing expressively and even sight-reading written notation more fluently. Encouraging students to listen first rather than immediately rely on written music strengthens their overall musicianship, making them more adaptable and confident players.

For children who naturally gravitate toward learning by ear, it's important to embrace this strength rather than discourage it when they start working with written music. Instead of forcing them to rely solely on notation, teachers and parents can use auditory learning as a bridge, encouraging students to listen to recordings, sing melodies before playing them, or even write down rhythms and notes they hear. Rather than seeing ear-based learning and reading music as opposing skills, students benefit most when these two abilities support each other.

There are many simple and engaging ways to cultivate strong auditory skills in all students:

- **Call and response games** – Play or sing a short musical phrase and have students echo it back.

- **Finish the melody** – Start a song and let students hum, sing, or play the next phrase based on what they hear.

- **Sing what you play, play what you sing** – Encouraging students to match their voice to their instrument strengthens their ability to recognize pitch and phrasing.

- **Imaginary performances** – Ask students to close their eyes and "hear" a song in their head before playing it, reinforcing their ability to recall music internally.

By developing strong listening skills, students gain a deeper connection to music, become more expressive players, and develop confidence in their ability to learn new pieces in multiple ways. Whether they prefer to learn by ear or through notation, both paths help shape them into well-rounded, independent musicians.

Compared to language development, ears are the ability to understand spoken language.

EYES - Reading

Reading music, part of the broader concept called "music theory" or the "grammar" of music, usually involves reading and writing using music notation. Not every musician reads music, and some read music written down without traditional Western notation on the musical staff (for instance, bands that play using Tabs or chord charts). Having written tools is less necessary for some musicians now that music can be recorded so easily on smartphones and computers, but it still does help create a common language that lets musicians enter different musical "worlds."

This is a valuable skill that helps children become more independent and confident musicians, even if they prefer to learn by ear or through movement. While some young musicians are naturally drawn to visual learning—finding it intuitive to recognize patterns on the musical staff—others may feel more comfortable relying on their ears or muscle memory at first. However, much like learning to read and write in a spoken language, developing fluency in written music opens up a world of opportunities and gives children a structured way to deepen their musical skills over time.

Written notation allows children to see music systematically rather than a series of memorized sounds or hand positions. It provides a way to understand patterns, recognize relationships between notes, and connect what they hear to what they see on the page. This strengthens their ability to play new songs more easily, communicate with other musicians, and eventually explore more complex music with confidence. Even if a child starts by playing simple songs by ear, gradually introducing written music gives them the tools to decode rhythms, melodies, and harmonies independently, without always needing to rely on a teacher or recording.

Reading music links closely to music theory, or studying some of the formal rules of music. Some tools students use in addition to staff notation includes studying musical scales and chords by Nashville numbers (one to seven for the seven notes of a scale) or solfege names (do- re- mi). Reading skills are often the most highly emphasized in traditional or academic music study, but it is just one of the three major components that music makers will need to be active music participants

Of course, learning to read music takes time, and some children may resist it if they find it challenging at first. The key is to introduce it gradually and in engaging ways so that it feels like an extension of their musical experience rather than an academic task. Some effective ways to build music-reading skills include:

- **Matching sound to symbol** – Encouraging students to sing or play a familiar tune while following along with written notes helps them connect what they hear to what they see.

- **Using movement and games** – Clapping written rhythms, tracing notes in the air, or playing "musical scavenger hunts" with notes and symbols makes the process active and fun.

- **Chunking information** – Breaking music into recognizable patterns (such as measure by measure or line by line) makes it feel manageable, just as children learn words and phrases before reading full sentences in a new language.

- **Combining ear training with notation** – Encouraging children to write down simple melodies they've played or sung helps them see how written notation represents the sounds they already know.

While some young musicians may prefer to play by ear or use alternative notation systems like chord charts, a strong foundation in reading music ultimately makes them more well-rounded and adaptable musicians. It allows them to engage with a wider range of musical styles, collaborate more easily with other musicians, and develop a deeper understanding of how music is structured. Even if reading notation isn't a child's primary way of learning at first, introducing it as part of their musical journey ensures they have the tools to grow, explore, and express themselves fully through music.

Just like learning to read a language, eyes are used to develop the understanding of written music.

Putting it All Together

"Learning Music" is actually a large umbrella for several major skills, that include processing information and responding through most of the major senses. Music lessons should ultimately provide a balance of three things:

1. Easy, Comfortable Playing (Touch/Technique):
To play music well, students need to know how to move their hands and bodies in ways that feel natural and healthy. We teach the skills that help them play with ease, control, and confidence, so they can focus on making music, not just getting the notes right.

2. Listening Like a Musician (Ears/Listening Skills):
Strong listening skills help students hear the details in music—like rhythms, melodies, and harmonies—so they can

play more accurately and with expression. We teach them to trust their ears, making it easier to pick up new songs and bring music to life.

3. Understanding How Music Works (Eyes/Theory & Knowledge):
Music has its own rules, patterns, and language that help everything fit together. We show students how to read, understand, and make sense of music, giving them the tools to learn new songs faster and even create their own.

Key Takeaways

- Music is a full-body experience, integrating visual, auditory, and kinesthetic learning.

- Each child has a dominant learning style, and recognizing and making it primary can make their musical journey more natural.

- Over time, children should develop flexibility in all three learning modalities to become well-rounded musicians.

- We can use a variety of tools to help children use one sense (such as auditory cues) to help them practice other sense (like music reading)

What's Next

Strong musical roots—whether built through touch, listening, or reading—give children the foundation they need to grow as musicians. But what happens next? What does that growth actually look like? Just like in a garden, where strong roots don't guarantee identical flowers, every child's musical journey unfolds in its own way. Some will dive deep into performance, others will use music as a creative outlet, and for many, the value of music will show up in unexpected ways—boosting confidence, shaping critical thinking, and even influencing how they navigate the world. In the next chapter, we'll explore the bigger picture: how music education connects to lifelong growth, opportunity, and the skills that truly matter—not just in music, but in life.

CHAPTER SIX

Growth and Opportunity

"Music acts like a magic key, to which the most tightly closed heart opens." – Maria von Trapp

Things I Worry About

I am a parent. I worry about my kids like every parent does. I wonder what they will need in order to be successful (and happy) in life.

How will they compete in the economy of the future? How will they manage their own mental wellness? What skills will they need?

I wonder how technology is affecting them now in their mental health and development, and how they will interact with technology in the future, both in their careers and their personal lives.

In 2021 music lessons took a surge at our school. Families were less busy as many activities or locations still faced shutdowns or restrictions and the need for human connection and creative outlets were very tangible. Making music served people very well during a difficult time.

Then something changed. Things went "back to normal" and we all got busy again. Why, in the face of so much research that music education provides vital benefits, does it get put up on the shelf so easily?

In a garden, it is hard to get a guaranteed outcome. Imagine starting out with the desire to grow a prize-winning largest pumpkin of the year. You can only be sure that you will grow a pumpkin, but you will never know if it will be the heaviest one until the end of the season. It is hard to be patient in the face of such uncertainty. But there is no other way. Investing in growing things always yields fruits, but you cannot promise exactly what each harvest will look like. I hope to provide some encouragement about what kind of harvest you can hope for.

This chapter will dispel the industrial, or carpenter, based ideas that promise a certain set of results, and instead suggest that by committing to the creative process we can be sure that the artist will grow, even if any one piece of art they create may be or not.

"I Guarantee It"

As I mentioned, I grew up in the 80s and early 90s, where iconic commercials guaranteed results, along with other iconic catchphrases like "Got Milk?" and "I've fallen and I can't get up!" Maybe the 90s were not unique in that way. My social media feed today is full of people making promises to make me richer and more fit. It's really tempting. Artists have progressively fed into the same funnel: you either are a "success" or a "failure" as a musician. Everyone that does not win on a reality talent competition is, by definition, a "loser" to that system. The pressure to be a "good" musician, or even worse a "successful" musician, is stifling. The first chair in the band or orchestra section is the best. The lead singer is more important than the back-up singers. Fame matters, money matters.

Except it doesn't. **Being creative and expressive matters.**

Most parents I speak with don't really want their child to become a career musician. But the model of winners and losers is subtly set for everyone.

- "Either you start practicing more or I am getting rid of the piano"

- "They haven't been making progress (aka finishing a book of lessons or passing an annual exam) so we are going to stop doing music"

- Or lots of varieties of "We are too busy" (again usually a "not enough results" driven statement)

Sometimes, it is true, students get bored or do not practice enough.

But maybe, just maybe, they are the victim and not the perpetrator in that crime. They may not be "losing" at the game of music. They may just be unfulfilled.

Don't get me wrong. I am not telling you that unless you keep spending more month over month on a professional music teacher that you are doing something wrong. Teachers are great tools, but we are not the gatekeepers of music. The pathway of making music is open to anyone and should be free.

I would ask this: "making" is ok. Make music. Any kind of music.

I know this is not an easy ask. I remember teaching Morgan when he was 8 years old, and once he learned the "Cantina Band" from Star Wars (which would not have been my first pick for his abilities at the time) he was obsessed. After weeks of the phenomenon, his dad approached me and said he seriously considered getting rid of the piano if he heard the song one more time.

Morgan was not winning on a traditional trajectory. He was, however, experiencing joy and a state of flow–being so immersed in his art in a feeling we all seek (but sometimes find more dangerously through drugs and other substances and other risky behaviors).

Here is the thing. Music, and all creative endeavors I believe, are not "winning" sports.

What Kind of Sport Is This?
(Music vs. Competitive Culture)

This is like the soccer games I signed my kids up for when they were four. No one kept score. Ok, I admit I was tempted to sometimes, but the idea that we should be winning all the time is REALLY strong. We were supposed to be there to help a growing little human develop healthy habits and have fun getting exercise, practicing teamwork, learn some new skills and figure out if this activity brought her joy. Making things, especially music, should be the same way.

Imagine if we all enrolled our preschoolers in soccer only to find out if they were "good enough" to "be sports people" for their life. And if they did not work hard enough or make enough progress, they were out. Is that the true purpose of sports? If so, we should really stop calling them "games." But if anyone can play–and benefit from their time playing, win or lose–then a game it is.

Of course there are professional musicians just as much as there are professional athletes. Let's remember, though, that for 99% of us it is the journey, not the destination that matters. Making music is a journey and you are not on the winning or losing side.

You are winning though - if you stay in the game. Too many people quit, or get chased out, of their own creativity. This is not just true of music: after about the age of 10 most of us either imagine our drawing is going to be "good enough" to be professional one day, or we stop showing it to anyone and keep it very private. We either join a dance team, or stop dancing for other people to see, that is, until we are old enough to drink enough to bring it back out. The real loss is when we judge ourselves, or our children, that either we have to be "really serious" or nothing at all.

The goal is just to stay in the game. As a teacher I am not looking for students that won the golden ticket for musicianship. Everyone has a ticket, they just need permission to ride. Keep creating. Help our children be brave. Encourage them to play music they love and share it with family and friends (be wary of the internet, which will quickly sort art back into winners and losers for no good reason). Make art a trusted friend. Not the judgy friend that makes you always worry if you are really good enough. Make it the friend that you have with you for life. Music can be that friend.

Sometimes parents tell me that kids learn things from sports that they don't learn in the arts. Respectfully, however, I think there are parallels in both we can learn from. Music is like golf. Golf is a solo pursuit of perfection. This is a prevailing mentality in the classical/traditional world of music teachers, to achieve the best performance possible

Music is also like soccer. Soccer is a team sport where all the practice hinges on the ability to win at game time. It requires teamwork, but also has a hierarchy of important positions and awards most valuable player awards. This is the common mentality behind rock or popular music teachers.

You don't have to just choose one—you can get the benefits from both solo and group efforts. My point here is that there are different things to be gained on the musical journey, especially if you stay "in" long enough to really explore. I took private lessons for a long time before I ever, very hesitantly, joined a band at church with my peers. Other students picked up their instrument at school and have always played in a group and the idea about performing a solo is terrifying. There are solo and group elements we can experience, and we can "win" as a soloist or as a group—but more than winning, we can GROW from both types of experiences.

The debate about the value of competitive elements in creative education is not new. Composer Bela Bartok is quoted in a newspaper article from 1962 about the value (or damage) a competitive environment brings. **"Competitions are for horses, not artists."**

Eat Your Vegetables

Broccoli is not typically the most fun you can have on a plate. Neither is practicing every day. And there are artificial rewards for eating broccoli—we have all done it. "Eat your vegetables and you can have some ice cream." There is nothing wrong with that in my opinion. But the broccoli itself did not produce the ice cream. Broccoli produces something else for you.

It produces good health over time. It makes you a lot happier when you are 60 and more healthy and active then your peers. It gives you energy to live a full life, it cannot guarantee good health but it sure can help. It doesn't get a lot of credit. Also, if you eat broccoli for a month you won't lose 20 pounds or gain big biceps. It is a part of a lifestyle with real benefits but without quick wins. Out with instant gratification, in with good old working on something and seeing it become a reality.

I believe we have to shift our mentality. We don't study math, eat vegetables or even learn to go to potty on the toilet because

- It's always fun

- I am naturally talented at it

- I will become famous doing it

Instead, we do these things because they are important things we need to grow up and participate in society. They give us tools for a healthy or successful life, even if we don't grow up to be an engineer or an athlete. Music is another tool in that tool belt.

It is not so much about the music or art our children can create as it is about what music and art creates IN our children.

The Practice of the Process
(not the Production of Perfection)

I like keeping my children safe. Being creative is not a "safe" pathway because we cannot control the success or failure of how others respond to our talent or ideas. We can only control the work we put into it.

Seth Godin writes about what he calls "The Practice" The idea of The Practice is all about showing up consistently, trusting the process, and focusing on the work rather than the outcome. He says that being creative or successful doesn't come from waiting for inspiration to strike or chasing perfection. Instead, it's about building habits that allow you to do the work, day after day, without being overly attached to whether it's "perfect" or not.

It's not just about the concert and the recital. We don't have to wait until we are "good enough" to play. Instead we can help our artistic students to finish a project, perform it, and move on instead of expecting perfection. It's about encouraging your child to embrace the process of learning—to practice, try, make mistakes, and try again. This is why I think that music makers are so brave. Godin reminds us that failure and feedback can also be stepping stones to growth, and the magic happens when we stay committed and moving forward, even when it feels hard or uncertain.

Godin also emphasizes that creativity isn't reserved for a lucky few; it's something everyone can cultivate. He calls us to let go of the fear of being judged or failing and instead to focus on putting our work out there for others. For kids, that might mean performing at a recital or sharing their artwork. For parents, it's about modeling that mindset—showing them that consistent effort matters more than instant results.

Show up, do the work, and over time, you'll see growth, creativity, and confidence blossom.

"Writers write. Runners run. Establish your identity by doing your work."– Seth Godin, The Practice

Music and Life Skills

How many of these traits do you want for your child? I know many of these qualities are incredibly important to me, even more than my child's GPA or future career choices. These are some of the many qualities that children can practice while learning to sing or play a musical instrument.

1. **Clarity and Focus:** Successful people have a clear vision of their goals and stay focused on achieving them. They consistently prioritize tasks that help them accomplish their goals.

2. **Positive Mindset:** Maintaining an optimistic attitude helps successful students overcome challenges. The habit of practicing music helps children view setbacks as learning opportunities and stay resilient in the face of adversity.

3. **Continuous Learning:** Lifelong learning is a key trait. Successful people seek knowledge and skills to adapt to changing environments, staying ahead in their personal and professional lives.

4. **Discipline and Consistency:** Making music is much more about long term work than about making short term gains

5. **Strong Work Ethic:** Successful people dedicate time and energy to their endeavors. Hard work and determination, like learning to play music, are central to achievements.

6. **Adaptability and Flexibility:** We want our children to embrace change and adjust strategies when necessary. Being open to new approaches allows them to stay innovative and effective.

7. **Effective Communication:** Strong interpersonal and communication skills help students build meaningful relationships and collaborate with others productively.

8. **Confidence and Self-Belief:** Believing in their own abilities motivates people to take calculated risks and pursue ambitious goals.

9. **Value of Relationships:** Most music requires a team effort, like every choir, band or orchestra member has experienced. Musicians learn that their part

belongs in a whole and then tend to tolerate, appreciate and value working with others.

10. **Time Management:** Prioritizing tasks and avoiding distractions, which students can experience in daily practice, helps them maximize productivity and achieve work-life balance.

11. **Gratitude and Generosity:** Success comes with expressing gratitude for achievements and giving back to the community, fostering a sense of purpose and fulfillment. Creative children develop generosity when they share their art and perform it for others.

12. **Passion and Purpose:** Helping a child who loves music to align their work with their passions, helps them find the same motivation and satisfaction in their future endeavors.

Music and Brain Health

Beyond these character qualities that music helps build, research consistently shows that musical training physically shapes the developing brain in powerful ways. When we are making music we are promoting brain growth and holistic development.

1. **Musical Training Changes the Brain:** Learning to play an instrument or engaging in musical activities leads to changes in the brain's structure and function. This includes the reorganization of gray matter and

improved connectivity between different brain regions.

2. **Enhances Cognitive Abilities:** Musical training improves a variety of cognitive functions such as memory, attention, and problem-solving skills. It strengthens the brain's ability to process both auditory and non-auditory information.

3. **Boosts Neuroplasticity:** Studies highlight how music fosters neuroplasticity—the brain's ability to adapt and change throughout life. This is particularly beneficial not just in childhood but also in adulthood, aiding in lifelong learning.

4. **Improves Sensory-Motor Skills:** Musicians show enhanced coordination between sensory input (like hearing) and motor output (like finger movements), making them better at tasks that require precise timing and control.

In simple terms, research shows that music isn't just about entertainment; it actively shapes the brain, making it more adaptable, smarter, and emotionally attuned. For references, see research links at www.newsongsmusic.com/manual.

Key Takeaways:

- Creativity isn't a luxury—it's a skill set that prepares children for happiness and success in an unpredictable world.

- Music teaches both independent problem-solving and collaborative teamwork, essential for future opportunities.

- The goal of creative education isn't a perfect product, but a lifelong ability to create.

- Creativity flourishes best in an environment that values process over results.

- Feedback that affirms the work, not the results, can help build continued confidence

What's Next

Growth in music—and in life—is rarely linear. It doesn't come with a straight path or a guaranteed outcome, but instead unfolds through exploration, persistence, and the willingness to embrace the unknown. In the last chapter, we looked at how music education fosters opportunity—not just in developing musicians, but in shaping adaptable, resilient, and creative individuals. But how does that growth actually happen? What does the process of learning music look like, beyond just "practice more" or "get better"? In the next chapter, we'll dive into *The Learning Cycle*—a dynamic, ever-evolving process of imagining, practicing, and sharing. Because when students understand that learning isn't a race to perfection but a continuous cycle of growth, they're far more likely to stick with it—and to carry those lessons into every part of their lives..

CHAPTER SEVEN

The Learning Cycle

Music, like the brain, is a complex web of interconnected things, including physical skills, processing auditory information, learning to read music and understanding it's theory or grammar, and many more simultaneous processes. We cannot master music one thing at a time–it's not possible to first learn all the physical skills and then move on to the listening skills, etc. They are all being refined and built side by side.

This is why I refer to learning as a cycle. You don't begin and end a skill, you "level up" constantly. If we are moving around and around through the cycle, it can be difficult to mark the achievements that students have made. I think of the process in three parts, and they are all essential to help students (of any age) feel like they are making progress. Notice that one of the stages is "practice", which sometimes is the only phase that we focus on with students. Instead of measuring practice alone, there is a cycle of imagination, which opens a student up to a new skill and idea, then practice to refine or master that idea, and finally sharing to cement that new skill into place, make it relevant, and help students catapult forward into their next stage of imagination.

IMAGINE

"The best teachers are those who show you where to look, but don't tell you what to see." — Alexandra K. Trenfor

Visualizing

The first is that I want students to "picture" themself as a musical person. Capture a vision of the future. Why are we doing all of this hard work? Resilience and determination are much stronger when we are working towards a personally significant goal. A child that wants to be on stage should be able to learn music that will win the admiration of their peers at the talent show. Teachers and other adults also should also help students understand a wide world of music. For instance, I do not know a lot of children that can "picture" themselves playing jazz, many teens get inspired after being exposed to jazz by their teachers.

Improvising

The second way I use the term imagine involves exploration, or the "Improvisation" step in the Music Learning Theory. I actually grew up as a music student very afraid of musical improvisation. I learned only in retrospect, how valuable it can be to have to make my own musical decisions and the freedom that is developed from playing my own music.

Successful improvisation is not just "play whatever you want, ok ready...go." Very few students thrive that way. Instead, like asking kids to complete a single step (like, pick up the Legos and put them in the box) before giving them a large task (go clean your room), we also give students specific parameters.

I like to help students imagine their instrument with similarly small creative jobs. Pick three notes. Make a little song. Use your imagination. .

Flow

Imagination can open the door to students experiencing the immersive impacts of the "flow" state. Research into the flow state, such as Mihaly Csikszentmihalyi in "Flow: The Psychology of Optimal Experience" says "Flow is a subjective state that people report when they are completely involved in something to the point of losing track of time and external concerns." Starting with the imagination, whether it is dreaming up a brand new song or sounds, or dreaming of yourself performing a favorite song, helps students feel more completely involved in what they are doing. This is the first step to experiencing a flow state.

This kind of flow is active, not passive. My children and your children, along with you and I, are constantly invited into more passive forms of entertainment (hey, I appreciate binge watching shows as much as the next person). But this flow state is a different experience altogether. **Csikszentmihalyi says, "The best moments in our lives are not the passive, receptive, relaxing times... The best moments usually occur if a person's body or mind is stretched to its limits in a** voluntary effort to accomplish something difficult and worthwhile."

Getting really immersed into music sets up students for the next step in the cycle–the hard work of practicing to bring your imagination into reality.

PRACTICE

"When we focus on what we're doing, the experience becomes intrinsically rewarding, even if it is difficult." Daniel Goleman – Focus: The Hidden Driver of Excellence

Nearly every parent with a child studying music can worry sometimes (or most of the time) about if their child is practicing enough or adequately. Practice is definitely essential, but it also should not remove the joy, connection and curiosity that making music provides.

Focus on Quality Over Quantity

Practicing with intention and focus, even for shorter durations, can lead to more significant improvements and a deeper understanding. Consistency is the bedrock of any successful practice routine. Just like watering a plant fosters its growth, regular practice nourishes the developing skills of young musicians. It's not about spending hours on end every single day, but rather about creating a routine that's both manageable and effective. To cultivate a love for music, aim for short, daily sessions that fit comfortably into your child's schedule, ensuring that practice becomes a natural part of their life rather than a burdensome chore. Each day's effort builds on the last, turning challenging pieces or techniques into familiar friends.

Set Clear Goals

One of the keys to effective practice is setting clear and achievable goals. Whether it's mastering a challenging passage, improving tone quality, or learning a new piece, having specific and measurable objectives can provide direction and motivation during practice. Encourage your child to set short-term and long-term goals, and celebrate the milestones they achieve along the way. This deliberate approach not only makes practice more purposeful but also more rewarding, as your child can clearly see their progress toward their musical ambitions.

Emphasize Problem-Solving and Self-Reflection

Learning to navigate through challenges and obstacles is an essential skill in music and in life. Encourage your child to develop problem-solving strategies when they encounter difficult passages or technical hurdles. This can include slowing down the tempo, breaking down the music into smaller sections, or using different practice techniques such as chunking, looping, or varied rhythms. Teaching effective problem-solving strategies fosters independence and resilience in young musicians.

Reflection is a powerful tool for improving performance and

learning from past experiences. Encourage your child to think about what went well and what could be improved next time. This mindfulness fosters an adaptive mindset; they learn to critique their performance constructively and make informed decisions about their practice going forward. Children who understand that adaptability is a part of the learning process are more likely to confront challenges with resilience and determination.

Utilize Technology and Resources

Incorporating technology and various resources into practice sessions can make learning more engaging and effective. Tools such as metronomes, tuning apps, and recording devices can aid in developing a better sense of rhythm, pitch accuracy, and self-assessment. Additionally, online tutorials, educational apps, and interactive learning platforms can provide supplementary resources to enhance practice sessions and inspire creativity.

Celebrate all kinds of Progress

Lastly, it's important to create a positive and enjoyable practice environment. Incorporate elements of fun, creativity, and exploration into practice sessions to keep your child engaged and motivated. Recognize and celebrate their efforts and progress with praise, encouragement, and small rewards.

It's important to remind young learners – and ourselves –

that mastery does not happen overnight. Emphasize to your child the value of patience and the beauty of slow but steady progress. **Progress can be subtle**, and they might not notice it daily, but over time, they will be able to look back and appreciate the journey they've been on.

It's an opportunity to instill in our children a growth mindset when it comes to practice. Emphasize that mistakes are opportunities for learning and growth, and not indicators of failure. With a positive attitude towards challenges and setbacks we can help our children develop resilience and perseverance in their musical journey. One of the best ways to celebrate progress is to share it with others, demonstrating that your work is valuable enough to show others.

SHARE

"Having a healthy amount of connection capital leads kids to feel confident, capable, safe, and worthy." - Dr Becky Kennedy "Good Inside"

Sharing musical experiences is a wonderful and natural way to "complete" a cycle of learning and help students move ahead to new challenges. Music should encourage connection and helping students share musical experiences (and progress) with others should be a regular part of their experiences.

This does not mean that all students need to enter a high-pressure performance environment. Competitions, evaluations and recitals are all common "sharing" experiences for music students, and some students thrive there. Others do not, but that does not mean they should not seek out other opportunities to share their musical experience with others.

Our brains include a very cool feature called mirror neurons. Mirror neurons are one of the biological ways we know that we are "hard-wired" to share connections with others. They are specialized brain cells that fire both when we perform an action and when we observe someone else performing the same action, helping us understand others' intentions and emotions. These neurons are thought to play a key role in learning, empathy, and social interaction by allowing us to "mirror" the experiences of those around us. Mirror neurons work when we watch people play on YouTube–but not in the same way. When we share "in person", or even on live video feeds such as Zoom or Facetime, which rank lower than live meetings but higher than video recordings when it comes to mirror neuron activity, our brains learn in a more powerful way.

Music offers many opportunities to play with and for other people and to mirror their actions, and even their smiles. There is a lot of hard work that happens alone when students practice, but music also needs to come out of the practice room and into the community.

There are many ways to share in a community other than traditional performances. Encourage your child to attend workshops, join an ensemble, or participate in local music events. These experiences provide a sense of camaraderie and shared passion that can be incredibly inspiring. They also offer practical opportunities to apply what's been practiced in a social and supportive environment, which can significantly enhance learning and retention. Communities can be small, such as a private music teacher, or large like a community band or orchestra, it could include peers or could be a mix of ages, may come from your family or from outside the home. Finding a community helps complete the learning cycle and restart the imagination to help the growth spiral continue.

A Musical Community Helps Students:

1. **Accepting constructive feedback:**

When you share your musical journey with others, you open the door for constructive feedback that can help you improve and grow. Whether it's a technical element of your playing, an interpretation of a musical piece, or advice on performance anxiety, the insights from others can provide a fresh perspective.

2. **Setting goals with accountability and tracking progress:**

When you share your musical journey, you open the door to set specific goals. This level of accountability can be motivating and provide direction for your practice and overall improvement as a musician.

3. **Feeling a sense of belonging:**

By connecting with fellow musicians, you can feel a sense of belonging within a community who shares your passion for music. This sense of belonging can be incredibly empowering, especially during challenging times in your music journey when you may feel isolated or discouraged.

Being part of a community of musicians allows for the sharing of inspiring stories, challenges, and successes. The encouragement and inspiration offered by others can drive you to overcome challenges and strive for new heights in your music.

4. **Nurturing a love for music**

A mentor who is focused on personal growth understands that success in music is not solely about perfecting technique. They will introduce students to a variety of musical styles and encourage creative expression, allowing students to explore and find their own voice. Their teaching methods aim to inspire a lifelong love and appreciation for music, rather than just preparing for the next performance or examination.

Building connections with others provides a source of support and understanding. You can share experiences, exchange tips, and offer encouragement to one another, creating a collaborative and supportive environment in which everyone can thrive. These experiences can expand your musical horizons and contribute to your growth as a musician.

You have the opportunity to both give and receive feedback, fostering a sense of accountability to your musical pursuits. Mutual support encourages a spirit of collaboration and continuous improvement in your musical journey.

Teaching Resilience Through Music

A significant part of personal growth is learning to overcome obstacles. A supportive mentor knows that setbacks and plateaus are natural components of learning and will provide strategies to help students navigate these challenges. They will teach resilience by showing how to learn from mistakes, adapt to different situations, and persist through difficulty.

One sign of a mentor who values personal growth is their encouragement of autonomy in their students' learning process. They will guide their students to become self-sufficient musicians who can set their own goals, assess their performances critically, and pursue their musical interests with curiosity and independence. Such **autonomy is empowering**, cultivating a sense of ownership over the musical journey.

A mentor focused on the holistic development of a student recognizes the importance of community and connection in music. They encourage ensemble play, collaborations, and participation in music events, fostering a sense of belonging and team spirit. These experiences are invaluable, as they teach social skills, empathy, and communication within a musical context.

"**Connection is the opposite of shame.**" - Dr Becky Kennedy "Good Inside"

Key Takeaways

- Learning music isn't a factory or inputs and outputs

- Music is a "living" cycle of creativity, learning, and growth.

- Imagination and experimentation give students creative autonomy.

- Practicing music is about more than discipline—it builds goal-setting and lifelong learning skills.

- Sharing music—in a variety of ways—keeps the cycle of learning alive.

What's Next

Learning is not a straight line—it's a cycle. We imagine, we practice, we share, and then we start again. But as anyone who has ever tried to learn an instrument (or stick with any long-term habit) knows, consistency is hard. The thrill of starting something new eventually meets the reality of effort, frustration, and plateaus. This is where motivation becomes the key to sustaining growth. In the next chapter, we'll have a look at how to keep the fire burning—not through forced discipline or empty rewards, but by tapping into the powerful forces of *autonomy, competence, and relatedness*. Because when music feels meaningful, when progress feels possible, and when kids feel in control of their own journey, they're far more likely to keep going—and that's where the real magic happens.

CHAPTER EIGHT

Staying Motivated

The real question we are all wondering about as parents is "How do I get my kids to practice?" Especially in an age of digital distractions, the focused work of practice is hard to do. Add to that the goal of making music a positive experience and not a shouting match, and the struggle is real. I wish I could wave Harry Potter's wand and "practicus happlius" kids into successful practice routines, I don't have that kind of magic.

I do recommend we take clues from the Self-Determination Theory (SDT) of psychologists Edward Deci and Richard Ryan. This theory suggests that we all need to practice autonomy over our choices and actions, feel competence in our ability to do the task we are given, and see the relatedness or relevance of the task. Without enough autonomy, competence and relatedness, kids turn to distractions for psychological nourishment.

Gamification is everywhere, from education to social media to, well, video games. I think there are lots of wonderful ways to use gamification in education. In an increasingly digital age, though, children are pulled away from the delayed gratification of guitar practice and into the instant gratification of Instagram. We can learn from the "hooks" that other games are placing and redirect them into more creative activities.

It's not easy, but we can use a variety of strategies to get over the hurdles and into the long-term vision we have helping our creative kids grow. It is common to start strong in music lessons and somewhere between month 3 and 9 it gets hard. No single strategy will carry us all the way through years of successful practice, just as no single garden tool can plant, weed, rake and water the budding plants. By having a variety of tools available as parents we are better equipped for all seasons.

On Motivation

Autonomy

Autonomy, or student-led learning, does not mean teaching without a plan or roadmap. One of the fears when giving students autonomy is that they will be lazy and select things that are easy, whether that is using easy skills such as choosing simple music reading tasks over learning more difficult sheet music, or easy choices such as learning a single comfortable and familiar genre without ever venturing out (such as students that would request to play only video game soundtracks)

These are valid concerns. Student autonomy does not mean that teachers arrive to a lesson without a plan or intention. Instead, they meet the student where they are.

As a teacher, I may plan to start at the beginning of the

method book and travel through to the end where a sonatina is sitting, ready to be performed. The child, however, may not be starting from the same place. People can enter the musical garden from many different places based on their unique skills and desires. If you are starting down a reading-based, classically focused path but the child arrives ready to use their music memorization skills to play popular songs, you may have a hard time traveling together.

Now let me tell you about Dominic. Dominic is a sweet, neurodivergent student who started making music with me in the preschool music class. Dominic did not travel the pathway of other students, who would participate in my planned activities and show me their mastery. He would observe, listen closely, and then choose to perform musical tasks at home and away from my view. I would accept his choice of actions in class, knowing that he was absorbing what he needed to and was indeed becoming more musical, even if he preferred to do it outside of the classroom setting.

As Dominic turned to school age, there came a time we were ready to transition from music class to piano lessons. My regular path to teaching a child to play the piano was well established—I had a variety of tricks up my sleeve to teach the physical/technical skills of classical piano playing, a successful tool for helping students read music, and then on to play a variety of chosen repertoire.

This pathway was not the way Dominic was going to travel. I would show him a piece of sheet music and guide him through. He would become quickly sidetracked to another task.

But if you listened to his "distractions" they were incredibly musical. He would sing me a variety of songs that he had been hyper-focused on that week. He would play melodies from movies and TV shows . They would typically be in the original key of what he had heard, no matter how many sharps or flats (mixing black and white keys) he needed to use. He connected what he "heard" in his mind to the keyboard. That was what I needed to use.

It can feel daunting as a teacher when you have to start down a whole new pathway you never needed to travel before. I grew up LOVING sight reading. Now I was going to teach for months or years with no books or printed music as all?

This is what inspired me. I cared about Dominic more than I cared about music. I wanted the best outcome for HIM, and not to measure him against myself or any other child.

So I gave him autonomy. If I showed up and he was singing songs from "Cinderella" I could join his pathway. We could work on that song together. What did I add? I challenged him to use all of his fingers in a more "traditional" way. I taught him how to harmonize a melody with chords. When we were ready we attached the song he was playing that week to a scale and practiced that. Occasionally we would play games about reading notes on the staff. And when we finished that, we went back to using his amazing ears to guide him around the piano, eventually he could play a variety of songs with both hands like most children his age would do, with or without their piano books.

Autonomy was having my own goals AND his goals in mind, and giving him freedom to make choices while we progressed together, starting right where he was. Using his own competence.

Competence

Next, competence means allowing students to do things they are GOOD at, and extending those skills bit by bit. Giving students a list of new things to do each week, things they just tried once or twice and require quite a bit more work to master, can be challenging. I am by no means asking all students to "slow down" or against setting high expectations. Instead, I suggest that students should feel a sense of mastery before they are sent home to play. We all like doing things we are good at.

I don't particularly like watching sports. Socially, I do not have other people in my life to enjoy it with. Practicing music all by yourself month after month is not nearly as inspiring as having music lovers in your life, just like it is more fun to watch the big game around other fans. It's great if you can sit down with a parent, grandparent or cousin and play together but it's also motivating to have another music lover just sit with you and enjoy music together, sing together, or listen to you perform...that is as long as you can perform things you feel competent doing. My youngest child discovered a love of sports, and so we watch together. My first football game I sat down to watch was not that enjoyable to me. It's not that there was anything wrong with the game. I just didn't understand it. I had no competence. I needed someone to explain the rules to me (slowly and without too much insider lingo—I always try to choose simple words whenever you can). Once I had mastered the rules of the game, it was fun to participate. Likewise, students should spend a majority of their time playing things that they feel CONFIDENT about doing, and then a smaller portion mastering something new. This can be the difference between music being a joy and music being merely more work.

Relatedness

Lastly, successful motivation requires relatedness. Some of the most compelling reasons I have as a parent for my child to practice: overall brain development, social-emotional learning, building discipline skills for life—are all irrelevant to an eight year old. There is little that they relate to about that. What CAN they relate to?

First: People. My motivation to watch football was all about relatedness, namely my relationship with my daughter. For many people, their favorite sports team is inherited from fathers or uncles, because it helps us feel connected. Music should have the same social connections. A child can set a goal to play the favorite song of someone they love, or add music to a special event. A child should have people that love to hear them play and celebrate their work.

Second: Interests. Music is found around the world and throughout time. It connects, we just need to find the ways that it does. Music can relate to a culture your family comes from, or just a culture that inspires you. Music from a favorite movie or game certainly feels like it relates to life.

And third: future goals. There are plenty of ways to open up students to explore, for instance, the music of Mozart, even if no one in their family does and it is not in their current interest. Take the time to answer "Why?". Why does this matter? It can connect to future goals such as entering a contest or evaluation. It can also connect simply to skills. For instance, "I know you liked playing the last song that was fast and exciting. This is a song that will also help us practice having fast fingers". Help a child to see that it all relates.

Giving students autonomy, competence and relatedness will set them up for much greater success. A child learning popular social media songs from YouTube videos has autonomy (they chose it), competence (assuming they choose something easy enough to master) and relatedness (they encounter the music in their everyday life). They lack, however, an experienced guide that can keep higher end goals in mind and help them continue to build their skills in a fun and functional way. Luke Skywalker focused only on the challenges directly ahead of him, it was Yoda who helped build step by step towards a much greater future than he could have imagined.

You Are Not an Algorithm

TikTok's "for you page" and YouTube's suggested videos have changed the way we receive entertainment. Children are given a feedback loop that continues to favor "more of the same" and discourages "try something new." Social media and online gaming platforms do not hide the model designed to keep people on their devices

The Hook Model

- **Trigger**: External or internal stimuli prompt an action.

- **Action**: The behavior performed in response to the trigger.

- **Reward**: A benefit, often variable, that keeps the user engaged.

- **Investment**: Effort put into the behavior increases the likelihood of repeating the cycle.

Our technology is full of triggers asking for the easiest possible actions with the high dopamine releasing rewards. Technology companies did not invent this model, but they have amplified it significantly.

The problem is many of us have more investment now placed in videos we have watched, things we posted, levels we achieved in our gaming platform, and less investment in being able to do things like play a musical instrument. These digital rewards feel good for a short time but lack the power to inform our children that they can be confident, creative people that can solve problems that lack obvious solutions.

Children are well aware of algorithms in their life. I heard a wave of six year olds who took up the phrase "don't forget to like and subscribe" when that was a key way YouTubers were gaining bigger audiences. They know a trending meme will get more likes than a thoughtful, personal or vulnerable statement shared with others. There is a formula to being popular, just like there are surefire ways to beat the final boss in Super Mario Bros. (OK, yes I am over 40 and this is what I know...)

Being authentic could easily be "cringey". It is safer to keep consuming the content that is similar to what you already liked in the past, and it is safer to present yourself in the ways that other people already liked in the past. We didn't all just wake up one day and decide to start all of our posted videos with "Hey guys..." We heard and imitated what everyone else was doing in their own online videos, unconsciously mimicking the crowd. The models that are getting presented follow the algorithm, not the ones being the most honest.

I don't want to sound too cynical. My own children groan when I tell them I have been researching online behavior trends in kids and teens. My kids (all teens or older at this point) do not have screen time restrictions. I am not trying to convince them that texting is bad, even though I still usually call instead of text. This is a nuanced problem and "ban screens" or anything like that is completely oversimplified and in my opinion not likely to work. I am not here to solve the internet.

I am here to suggest that we, and our kids, are MORE than our online activities, and that creative education is a big part of reminding and rediscovering those parts of ourselves. Viral performances are not better than all the other ones—they are just more seen.

Just to prove that more popular does not always mean best, there are many songs we love today that were not "viral" in their own time. The incredibly well-known song "Hallelujah" was not especially well known after its 1984 release on an independent record label. The first popular cover version was not recorded until 1991, followed by an even more popular cover in 1994. By the standards of social media it was a flop. But if they had never been created (or shared) we all would have missed out. You have cried at least once to a recording of "Hallelujah" haven't you?

There is a different kind of feedback loop we can create for our children. It is more challenging because there is a lot more work and a lot less instant success. Creativity and art are like that.

New Triggers for Authenticity

First comes the triggers. Young children have creative

triggers all the time. Ideas sprout out of nowhere. Over time many of us learn to ignore these impulses, but let's rewind and take time to celebrate crazy ideas.

Second, we can allow for action. Let's make creative actions safe and accessible to our children. Keep the piano (or, I know, even the drum kit) available where a child can sit down and try something when inspiration strikes. Keep scissors, glue and glitter handy at all times. Yes, I know I am asking for a level of chaos, mess and noise. But that is where art happens. Keep a notebook handy and give it over anytime your child is sharing something they thought about. Author Neil Pasricha says to his children that the only difference between writers and everyone else is that when writers have ideas, they WRITE THEM DOWN.

To pause for a moment, sometimes we have to help the triggers and the actions along the way. For all my students taking piano lessons, I want them to joyfully experiment with the piano when they have an idea. I also want them to do the work I have shown them to do in our weekly lesson. So there is a place for *created* triggers. The book Atomic Habits by James Clear has lots of amazing information on this topic. A trigger could be, "Before I get my iPad, I practice a song five times on the piano." The action could be playing the songs. Feedback loops can be planned the same way that seeds can be planted in rows or fertilizer and water applied at the right time.

We can cultivate CREATIVITY, not musical perfection, and

so we want to look for a variety of creative triggers and help them turn into actions.

Next, rewards. Wow there are lots of parenting books and blog posts and videos posted about theories of rewards and punishments. Every home can set their own rules, whether you "bribe" your children with stickers or you warn them that you will take away screen time—figure out what works for your household.

I would ask that you consistently recognize creative acts and give them some kind of reward. When your child wants to show you something they just figured out on the guitar, **stop and listen.** That is a reward. Tell them often that you are proud of them, especially for the work they did in practicing (not if the result was perfect or not). Invest into them–I would beg that you spend money to upgrade their musical instruments before you upgrade their technology sometimes. Playing on a "real" piano is a very real reward when you have been working on a small electric keyboard.

I know these things are not easy. Earning new skins on Fortnite or a score on the leaderboard or likes on your post are all cleaner, faster, cheaper and easier rewards than moving a two ton piano into your dining room or shopping for nice paints and an easel.

But we are more than our algorithms. Internet trends will measure if you create something with enough similarity to the last popular thing, and after 24 hours those likes and views all go away and you have to start over and win them back again.

Being a creative person is not about getting a few more likes today than you did yesterday. It is about finding an authentic voice, feeling your own feelings, making some art today that may be terribly bad and tomorrow something that is positively brilliant. Some creative work will never get seen by more than a few people.

Consider how "The Boy, the Mole, the Fox and the Horse" was created. The author and artist Charles Mackesy did not set out to make and post popular pictures. He doodled and sketched, and shared his work on WhatsApp with close friends and family when they could not see each other in person. He wrote and drew it because it was true to what he was feeling, not to see what was going to sell the most copies. Eventually, all of those rough sketches and ideas became a book, and that book became an award winning movie. It's an inspiring book and movie, and even a great origin story. But it did not come about because he created viral social media posts. He created art.

That action came with the reward of affirmation from family and friends. It also came with an internal reward–doing something you feel proud of. These actions stack up into investment. Invest in being a creative person. Invest in expressing yourself. Invest in trying to master something you are not sure you can do.

This feedback loop will end up far more rewarding than platinum level battle status or "going viral". It will also help us produce more truly great art in the world. It doesn't come easy, but if we as parents can invest, just as we ask our kids to invest, we can feed the creative feedback loop just as much as the dopamine loops our phones deliver every 60 seconds.

"I'll Just Learn It on YouTube"

There are many online courses available now.. There are some really great resources out there, and they can give students access to great ideas and education that money and distance would have prevented in the past.

But beware. There is a reason you don't (hopefully) just tell your kids that as long as they watch some math videos on TikTok they will be fine.

- The person "teaching" could be plain wrong
- They could be teaching the right thing at the wrong time (calculus videos are going to be frustrating if you haven't seen algebra yet)
- They may have different biases or priorities
- They could be ineffective (frustrating if you think "I just can't understand this"...when maybe THEY are just hard to understand)
- (This is a big one) there is SO much information

available, it is very hard to pick from

That is (hopefully) why you are reading this book. You are the best advocate and guide for your child's musical journey. You can partner with a great teacher to help curate that pathway. You can also curate it yourself–you know your child's dominant learning styles and interests and you are gaining a better sense of what being well-rounded looks like.

Music for a Lifetime

Ultimately, being flexible will help us support our kids as they grow and their needs change. Just like Dominic needed a different approach than my other students, your child's musical journey will have its own twists and turns. Whether you're just getting started with a five-year-old or helping a teenager refine their skills, the key is to remain responsive and keep joy at the center of the process. Music education isn't just about teaching notes and rhythms—it's about empowering our children to become creative people who can express themselves in meaningful ways.

Every child's musical journey is unique, just like every garden grows differently. What worked wonderfully for my daughter might not connect with my son, and that's perfectly okay. This might mean trying different practice routines, finding a teacher whose approach better matches your child's learning style, or exploring genres that spark their interest.

The beauty of this approach—grounded in autonomy,

competence, and relatedness—is that it creates an environment where our children can develop a genuine, lasting connection to music rather than burning out on someone else's expectations. When we stay attuned to our children's changing needs and interests, we help them build not just musical skills, but a creative identity that can bring them joy throughout their lives.

Key Takeaways

- **Autonomy**: Children thrive when they feel a sense of ownership over their creative journey.

- **Competence**: Carefully chosen tasks that students can succeed at helps them feel and show mastery. Mastery builds confidence, and confidence fuels further growth.

- **Relatedness**: Creativity should connect us to others and children should be able to find a meaning or purpose in what they are learning.

- **We can create "triggers"** that inspire children to express themselves authentically.

What's Next

Maintaining motivation is a process filled with challenges and rewards. Fostering autonomy, competence, and a sense of relatedness helps students stay engaged with their practice. However, motivation alone is not enough—students also need a clear roadmap to navigate the vast world of music. In the next chapter, we shift from the "why" of staying motivated to the "how" of expanding musical knowledge, ensuring that students develop both passion and direction in their learning.

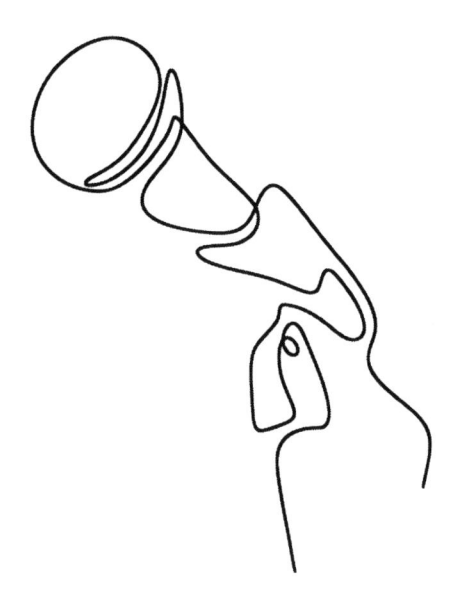

CHAPTER NINE

Sorting Out the Library

Picture walking into the Smithsonian Museum or the Library of Congress. You would have access to an almost unimaginable treasure trove of knowledge and experiences. You may feel excitement and anticipation, but you could also feel a sense of anxiety and overwhelm. That overwhelm would grow quickly if you were given some vague expectations about "working hard" and "making progress" without clear directions on how to get that done.

No one can learn all the music there is out there. But my hope is that most people don't camp out in front of a single shelf and ignore the rest of the library. One of the best ways to bravely venture out and explore the world of music is to have a map.

I was a good example of this growing up as a music student. I had some musical exposure as a 10 and 11 year old in school, but my formal music education (prior to college) consisted almost entirely of private piano lessons. I grew up in the classical tradition, learned to read music, and played primarily classical music, or played other genres as if they were classical (that is, using written sheet music).

Then one day in my teens I got a job. I think my dad somehow roped me into it (as he was known to do). My job was to play piano for the weekend for a kids musical theater workshop. So I showed up on Saturday morning to get my sheet music. Instead I got a handful of papers with lyrics and some chord symbols written on the top. The kids were coming in to sing in about 45 minutes. I panicked. It would be kind of like if I had been learning French for a few years and showed up to be handed a book in Spanish and asked to read it to the class. Luckily, I had done enough music theory worksheets that I could work my way backwards and survive the day. I don't imagine it sounded very good, but I got through it.

What had happened to me? I had crossed genres. I left the library shelf of historical novels and found myself in the cookbook section.

Let's be clear- neither historical fiction nor cookbooks are superior. Neither is "real" music over the other. They are just different, and we need to know what is out there and how to navigate without being intimidated if we want to enter a new area.

Genres: Who makes it, who gets it, and why did they make it.

Why do we love pop songs on the radio and movie soundtracks more than we love operas and sonatas (at least most people do). Certainly, we love their familiarity. But they were also written FOR us in mind. Understanding where music has come from can help students discover the relevance of music that feels unfamiliar to them.

Folk music is traditional or cultural music. Many times it has been handed down traditionally and may have no known author. These songs often have many variations, may appear at religious or other cultural events, and are often some of the easiest and most accessible. In recent days many times popular music has overshadowed folk music and we need to understand where it comes from.

"Art" or "Classical" music was traditionally written with a reason in mind, and understanding that reason can make the song more relevant. Mozart wrote to show off to rich patrons. Chopin wrote to try to introduce new sounds and emotions to a European audience. Tchaikovsky wrote music for ballet dancers to perform to. Churches, kings or universities often sponsored the creation of these songs.

Popular music was written for mass appeal. Art music does not necessarily have to be "popular", but Taylor Swift songs have to have lots of people that like to listen in and attend her concerts. Students should be able to compare how some songs are easy to sing along to, or easy to play, or have addictive "hooks" to get stuck in your head

Note: Music is a spectrum. There are endless variations in style and genre, so what I am about to present here is intentionally oversimplified. I would love for students to dive deep into what makes Thrash Metal different from Death Metal music. But these are baby steps to start from and so I purposefully selected only a few ideas to start with.

Who Makes It

"The Wheels on the Bus" is music. It is music when you watch it on YouTube and it is music when your grandmother sings it to you. "Pokerface" by Lady Gaga is music. It is music when she sings it at a live concert and it is music when your cousin sings it at karaoke. Mozart sonatas are music when at expensive symphony concerts and at free piano recitals.

Music is not just made by professionals. That is very important for us to understand and for us to communicate with our children. Music is democratic, it belongs to all of us, not just the ones that are best-paid, most famous or most "talented".

That being said, the question of "who made this" (primarily meaning who WROTE it, but also referring to who PERFORMED it) is a good first step to helping students understand what type of music they are encountering

Folk music: Who made it?

Folk music, as I define it most simply, is music that is not "owned" by any one person, and may easily change or adapt over time. It is accessible and shareable to everyone. Folk music is music that is shared freely by a community.

I define this also to include traditional religious music such as hymns (yes, they may have an author but are widely known and used by the community), and songs such as Twinkle Twinkle Little Star. Children I work with often associate such songs with media (recently, often referring to these songs to me as "Cocomelon" after the series on Netflix with these kind of nursery rhyme songs); instead of with their community (such as "songs my mother would sing to me"). By sharing the traditional nature of folk music with children, we allow them to see that there are not special qualifications you must have to make music, and that making music is open to everyone.

Pop music: Who made it?

Popular music, in a broad sense, is made by professional musicians, and in most cases these would also be considered "celebrity" musicians. Songs are associated strongly with the artist that first recorded them. This also includes music for "commercial" purposes such as soundtracks for TV, film and video games. Popular music is music written by an artist who wanted it to be popular.

In fact, there is a trend in some places to teach music entirely with this genre of music. It is familiar, generally rewarding to play because of other people's connections, and gets a lot of recognition when you perform it for others. When we are learning using popular music, I love to help students understand how popular artists were responding to the culture of the world around them, whether it was five months ago or fifty years ago. Popular music often has strong connections to history that students can discover.

Classical: Who made it?

I struggled with whether to call this last category "art" music or "classical" music. Art music could also mean "art for art's sake"- in contrast to the prior genres that were art for commercial success or for community uses. I am highly committed to helping children understand that they are a "real" artist no matter what kind of art they decide to make, so I decided against this direction. However, while I don't consider this type of music as the only "real art", I will keep the term classical music in the discussion to help us understand genres. Classical generally refers to historical Western "art" music. I would open this category up for classical music to also include historical professional music from around the world, not just the Western traditions, and also to modern day artists that are not writing for popular or mass media.

These classical musicians are generally highly trained and often work in the more academic realm or for public culture institutions like professional orchestras or opera associations. They are subject to professional critics, and usually want to create art that has some sort of lasting historical impact or communicate a unique artist's perspective about the world.

These composers and musicians can be some of the hardest ones for students to connect with naturally, so taking some time to explain their intentions can remind students that even music that is hundreds of years old was written by "real people" too.

Who is it for?

The intended audience is just as important as the person who created the music. If music is meant to be shared, we can better understand music in light of its intended audience.

Folk: Who is it for?

Folk music is unique--the creators and the audience typically can be one in the same. There is not a typical division of artist and audience, instead imagine a drum circle or a congregation singing. The group "receiving" the music is also the group making it.

Folk music can be a wonderful opportunity to discuss with your child if you have a cultural or family connection to a song. This can be as deep as sharing that you learned a particular song from a grandparent or another important relative, or as simple as sharing that a song like "Au Clair De La Lune" is in French, and sharing a friend that they know that speaks French. Making relevant connections to music, large or small, feeds a child's sense of connection.

Pop: Who is it for?

Popular music is made to appeal to a wide audience of people. It generally follows the expectations of the genre.

Popular music often hinges on commercial success, as artists rely on album sales and ticket revenues to sustain their careers. The ability to sell out concerts and rank on the charts is a sign of an artist's merit. Additionally, social media presence plays a crucial role in amplifying an artist's visibility and engagement with fans. In a competitive industry, maintaining popularity across these platforms can significantly influence an artist's overall success and longevity. The artist and the audience need each other, and generally this style of music is "for the fans"--and the more fans the better.

Talk with your children about experiences you have had with popular music, and also take the time to be a good listener. Most children have experienced popular music meant for fans their own age, and so listening to their favorite music can be a great chance to connect with them as well.

Classical: Who is it for?

Classical music historically was created for a sponsor or patron of some sort, or a group of patrons that agree to support the artist's message or intention

Art and music often flourish under the guidance of wealthier patrons who provide the financial support necessary for their creation and performance. These patrons may influence the direction and message of the art, dictating specific themes or ideas, though some artists are granted more creative freedom to explore their own visions. This dynamic results in a rich tapestry of works that can convey powerful messages or express complex ideas. Additionally, many artists and composers strive to preserve historically significant pieces, keeping cultural heritage alive while also showcasing the evolution of artistic expression over time.

I know many parents feel less personal connections to classical or art music, but these musical styles can also be a conversation starter about how the music makes your child feel or what they imagine. Usually this style of music was written to elicit feelings and images, so there are no wrong answers in discussion of what they imagine.

Why did you make it?

Finally, different types of music are written for different purposes.. Students can understand that they also have a purpose when they are making music, beyond just completing homework

Folk: Why did you make it?

Folk music is generally used in daily life to create shared experiences: Lullabies or work songs like sea shanties. They communicate a shared message, such as Afro-American spirituals. They generally serve as a connection point.

Folk music can provide an opportunity for students to understand that music can be a part of everyday life, and also appreciate that people from different times or places may have had different experiences.

There are also instances where this history may not be important (for instance, "Twinkle Twinkle Little Star" is hundreds of years old and has travelled around the world, but the history is pretty irrelevant for a child). Sometimes just appreciating the "passed down for generations" quality is quite enough.

Pop: Why did you make it?

Popular music is typically meant to be enjoyed. You can hear it in concerts or in recordings. It can be good for dancing too. It can send a message from the artist to their audience/fans, or be designed to give them specific feelings (like the scary music setting the mood for a scary movie). Classical and art music tends to be observed, while popular music usually invites more involvement. The audience is more likely to sing along or dance along.

Popular music can be a commentary of society as well, and can be a point of discussion and connection between adults and children about life in recent decades. Often popular music is also created for media such as video games and movies. Popular music can help students connect with the idea of being a "professional" musician if that is something they aspire to. Ultimately popular music is written to be catchy, memorable, and, well, popular.

Classical: Why did you make it?

Classical music is typically made to express an idea. The artist has an intention to communicate with others. They may want to innovate and so instead of following expected norms of the genre may specially challenge prior ideas.

If we travel back in history, one of my favorite examples is the classical sonata (or sonatina, which is just a little sonata). Sonatas are written in a very structured format (think of haikus or limericks in poetry: the structure is the same and then the topic or content is where the creativity shows) and I enjoy working with students to see the format. Sonatas start with the idea of a set form and then composers see what they can create within that form.

Another example would be to express an idea such as a character. Robert Schumann's "Album for the Young" has descriptive titles such as "The Wild Horseman" and "First Loss" that tell students exactly what the idea was. Other songs that don't have such literal titles give students an opportunity to determine for themselves the mood, idea, or character that they feel a song communicates.

Teaching and Learning Considerations

Folk Music

Folk music can have a powerful role in musical development.

- It is usually rhythmically and melodically simple, which enables students to internalize (or "audiate") music more easily and sing it with accuracy
- Once students have a strong inner sense of these shorter and simpler tunes they are useful to letting

students explore an instrument and discover tunes independently (as you may have witnessed a child "figure out" how to play "Mary Had a Little Lamb" on the piano, or using only 5 black keys anyone can play Old MacDonald–no music reading skills required)

- Folk music is full of variations, with songs often being sung slightly differently. This can open the door for students to improvise, or make their own creative changes to music, instead of feeling limited to playing it "exactly" right.

- Folk music is almost always harmonically simple, using a small number of chords, which also allows students to play a large number of "real" songs while practicing basic skills. For instance, using only two chords on a ukulele you can sing and play a large number of folk songs, giving lots of opportunities for practice (and success!)

"Common" folk songs will vary based on regions, culture, and family history. Here is a short list of folk songs to get your started that I use very commonly with 3 to 7 year olds, both for simply singing as well as for applying to instruments:

- Old MacDonald

- Hot Cross Buns (three notes, but note, I don't find many students have sung this in other contexts so I have to introduce it as a new song–I just tell them they are like cinnamon rolls when they laugh at the words "buns")

- Sally the Camel (or Alice the Camel) (three notes, for instance F, G, and A)

- Engine Engine Number Nine (three notes, for instance E, G, and A)

- Skip to my Lou (6 notes, but a relatively repetitive pattern of skips on a piano)

- The Farmer in the Dell (6 notes, but can be done on all black keys on the piano)

Nerdy Note: I generally use songs where notes work mainly in "steps" or moving one by one instead of making larger jumps between notes. Therefore a popular song like "The Wheels on the Bus" can be great for using chords/harmony early on but is harder to play melodically due to the number of skips or jumps between the notes. A teacher or parent with a little more musical training will have a better understanding of which songs are more "playable" in that sense, but don't let that stop you even if you don't have that knowledge, your instincts will often show you when a song has too many challenges for a child's current abilities.

Popular music

Popular music has its own place in the musical learning

materials. There is a whole genre of "rock schools" that have built their whole educational model around using popular (rock) music almost exclusively. There a a few things I like about popular music as a teacher:

- A lot of it is very accessible and helps students experience pride in playing "real" music relatively quickly. As I talked about in the garden discussion, helping students get "in" successfully is a key first step to helping them continue growing

- A lot of it is pattern based, and by finding and understanding patterns in music and making connections between songs students can get a deeper understanding of music

- It is great for sharing and social connections, and helps students enjoy performing more often and gets families involved by playing music others feel connected to

Students generally experience more internal motivation around popular music than other styles if they are unfamiliar with them

There are a few things I feel are important to using popular music successfully

- It can "teach to the test"-in other words lessons can focus on learning songs for the next performance and this rote based learning may not give students as many skills for being independent (for instance, there are some schools that discourage music reading or sheet music- but reading music will help students in the future be more independent learners and less dependent on a teacher)

- Rock musicians may need encouragement to feel comfortable getting outside the rock genres, for instance less likely to have the skills or knowledge to play hymns and church or in a jazz band at school (This can be true of traditional or classical players as well).

- Often this is called a "song based approach". Musical concepts are learned as they come up in the songs that are being learned. This can be a great approach but requires a tremendous amount of skill from the teacher to maintain a "scope and sequence" to music learning at the same time. More academic approaches will have a logical sequence: master quarter notes, then eighth notes, then sixteenth notes and syncopations. Song based approaches often require "skipping around" to the concepts as they appear in songs (and songs are often not presented from easiest to most difficult) so in "jumping around" it is easy to end up missing some key concepts. A great teacher will overcome this challenge, and encouraging a student to keep good notes of their own about things they have learned will help keep that knowledge available if they are not learning from a traditional music textbook

Popular music is a great resource to understand how music is combined out of several elements. Music has melody, it has harmony, and it has rhythm. Rhythms show up on the drums of the "rhythm section", separate instrument parts focus on just melody or just harmony and then the parts are combined, so the building blocks of a song can be more obvious.

Popular music is also great for "riffs". Similar to folk music, these can be shorter musical elements that can be easy to remember and play. I actually wish I had learned more about "riffs" when I was growing up as a classical piano kid–it would have been fun, relatively easy and encouraged listening and memorization. Popular music is not an all-or-nothing approach but is a huge part of every child's real musical experience as they grow it should also be a part of their musical education.

(Note that I am not going to discuss the age-appropriateness of popular music lyrics or themes. This is always a concern as well and please be aware of it. My favorite popular song for teaching is "The Lion Sleeps Tonight." It has all the easy elements of my favorite folk music too)

Art/Classical music

Classical music is already the centerpiece of *most* traditional music education, so many music lesson teachers, especially those that got a musical degree of some kind, tend to camp out in this style pretty easily. It is often "book-based" and encourages music reading skills when playing.

Since this is such a dominant tradition already, I will not discuss it here. As a classical piano teacher myself, I will be a "whistleblower" that sometimes when we teach other genres, we change the song but not the approach. There are "book based" ways to teach popular and jazz songs, but using the exact same sight-reading based approach one would use with Mozart or Beethoven. This is not the way a true rocker teaches popular music, and unfortunately some music teachers stay predominantly in one comfortable genre. Sometimes we "classical" musicians feel like the top of the food chain and don't have to play some of those "easier" forms of music, but being flexible and diverse helps all growing musicians be more well-rounded

Use the whole library

Parents, I ask that you actively help guide students through these decisions. Rock schools will look down on classical schools and vice versa, so please understand which style of music AND which styles of learning are going to help you student.

All types of music serve different purposes, and a focus on only one of these can limit students from their growth--whether it is focusing only on the familiar music of popular artists or sticking only the classical masterworks.

Instead, helping students see the various purposes music serves can help open them up to being creative participants instead of seeing a divide between themselves and "professional" musicians.

Key Takeaways

- Every genre has value—there's no "right" kind of music, only what speaks to each person.

- Exploring multiple genres deepens understanding and makes children feel less "lost" in the musical world.

- Helping children see the role of music in everyday life validates their journey as musicians, even if they're not professionals.

What's Next

Music is a vast and endless library—one that can feel both exciting and overwhelming. In the last chapter, we explored how understanding different genres, traditions, and approaches to music can help students feel less lost and more empowered in their learning. Now with a map to help guide the way around different styles of music, it is time to wrap up our discussion of why and how your child should grow musically. We will conclude with a reminder of the key things that making music produces—not fame and fortune, but connections, wonder and joy.

CHAPTER TEN

Conclusion

Some things I did not get to...

It is time to wrap this book up. We are all parents or caregivers together and I appreciate your time to read this far, when you could have been washing the dishes (or sleeping!) and it is not fair to make this story any longer.

Perhaps another day we can dive back into a few more important things that we did not discuss yet.

For one, music and mental health. I have made the case for music as a creative art and a place for creative play in our life. Along the way there are also skills with goal-setting and the discipline of exchanging instant gratification for the pride of mastering an instrument over time. There is also a lot of brain development, both in creating lifelong brain plasticity as well as brain synchronization, allowing our brain and ears to better work together. There is also a shared social bond through music.

Many of these elements affect mental health, but I want to acknowledge that there are many challenges our kids face in their mental health and music provides additional benefits specifically for self-care, self expression and positive mental health outcomes. Consider, for instance, that "We have new brain-based evidence that autobiographically salient music -- that is, music that holds special meaning for a person, like the song they danced to at their wedding -- stimulates neural connectivity in ways that help maintain higher levels of functioning." — Dr. Michael Thaut, University of Toronto.

For now, I will like to leave you with the fact that amongst music's many super-powers, improved mental health is yet one more reason to make music.

The second thing that I believe strongly in, but did not discuss, is the valuable role music plays with neurodivergent students. I work with a wide range of neurodivergent students, both diagnosed and undiagnosed, with a spectrum from ADHD to severe non-verbal impairments. Music truly "looks" different in all of these situations.

I believe that there are many ways students of all abilities can and should be active musical participants too, and there are many adaptive tools we have to help make that happen. That is, however, a discussion for another time. For now I want to share my conviction with you that music is by nature an inclusive activity.

Nurturing a Lifelong Relationship with Music

Music is more than an extracurricular activity; it's a profound tool for growth, creativity, and personal expression. Whether your child becomes a lifelong musician or simply carries a deep appreciation for the arts, the experiences they gain from learning music will shape them in meaningful ways.

The Value of Music Lessons

Music lessons offer more than just the ability to play an instrument. They help develop critical life skills such as discipline, patience, goal-setting, and problem-solving. Students learn to break down complex tasks, manage their time effectively, and embrace both successes and setbacks as part of the learning process. The cost of music lessons reflects not just the financial investment but the invaluable growth in cognitive, emotional, and creative development that comes with dedicated instruction.

Balancing Music with Life's Demands

Today's children are busier than ever, juggling academics, sports, social activities, and creative pursuits. While not every child needs formal music lessons throughout their entire childhood, every child can benefit from some form of musical engagement. This could be through structured lessons, participation in school music programs, or simply having access to instruments at home. The goal isn't perfection but fostering a positive relationship with music that fits into your child's unique life.

The Role of Parents in Music Education

You don't need to be musically trained to support your child's musical journey. Your encouragement, presence, and open communication are far more impactful than technical knowledge. Listening to your child practice, celebrating their progress, and maintaining an open dialogue with their teacher can make a significant difference. Additionally, families that learn and play music together often find it to be a source of connection and joy, strengthening bonds in unexpected ways.

Knowing When to Pause or Pivot

Deciding when it's time to stop or pause music lessons can be difficult. We recommend giving it at least a year, preferably 18 months, to allow children to move beyond the initial learning curve and experience the true joy of playing music. If a child isn't thriving despite trying different teaching styles, genres, or even instruments, it might not be the right time for formal lessons. However, this doesn't mean the end of their musical journey. Music can be revisited later when they're developmentally ready, or explored in other ways that suit their interests and strengths.

A Personal Reflection

As a music educator and parent, I've seen firsthand how varied and personal the musical journey can be. My own children have each carved out their unique paths—one thriving on stage, another finding joy in drumming despite minimal practice, and one channeling obsessive focus into guitar playing. Their experiences have reinforced what I've always believed: there is no one-size-fits-all approach to music education.

Whether your child becomes a performer, a casual player, or simply an enthusiastic listener, the goal is to nurture a lifelong appreciation for music. By providing opportunities, offering support, and respecting their unique interests, you help them build a relationship with music that can enrich their life in countless ways.

Final Thoughts

Music makes Connections

While getting distracted feels like an overwhelming trend, making it through the learning cycle gives students the ability to make music and feed their need for relatability. Music that lacks connection lacks life and is more likely to lead to frustration.

Connections means in one sense that music helps us feel bonded to others. We learn teamwork in orchestra and we activate our mirror neurons and synchronicity when we play duets. We build shared memories when we sing with others at home, or out at karaoke.

Connections also means we learn to see connections or relatedness in the world. Musicians recognize patterns in the world around them. They can find the link between Phil Collins "Groovy Kind of Love" and Clementi's Sonatina in F (if it makes you wonder, send me an email I will show you).

Music is Wonder-ful

Making music invites us to wonder. How can I perform this today? As a music maker, we don't have a fixed experience, where the recording sounds the same as it did the day before, but a growth based mindset where each day invites us to hear and try something new. Musicians more easily have a growth mindset, because the vast musical world always invites us to imagine songs we may play in the future, things that we can't do "yet" but are eager to work towards. In the words of Ted Lasso: "Be curious, not judgemental".

Music is Joyful

Making music, especially in an environment with "sharers" instead of "winners", brings noticeable smiles to both the music makers and their listeners. Music is fun. It fills many of our happiest memories. Let's encourage children that are free to sing, free to dance, and free to participate in music without fear that they are not good enough.

APPENDIX

Questions & Answers

When parents consider enrolling their child in music lessons, it's natural to have questions and concerns. Life is busy, resources are limited, and every child is unique. Some parents worry about the cost and time commitment, while others question whether their child is truly "musical" or if they'll stick with lessons long enough to make it worthwhile. Many wonder if they have the knowledge or ability to support their child's practice at home.

This chapter is designed to address those very concerns. My goal is to provide thoughtful, practical insights based on years of experience as a music educator and parent. Whether you're worried about balancing music with other activities, unsure if your child has the right temperament or talent, or questioning the value of the investment, this chapter offers guidance and reassurance.

This chapter is here to help you navigate that journey with confidence, clarity, and an open heart.

Parent: I'm a little hesitant about signing my kids up for music lessons right now. We tried this with my oldest child a few years ago, and it didn't seem to go very well. Can I ask, what makes music lessons worthwhile for kids like mine who are already juggling school and other activities?

Mr. Michael: I understand the hesitation about music lessons because I talk with lots of parents who have taken music lessons at some point in the past, and it didn't meet all their expectations. A common scenario is parents with a child in upper elementary or middle school who took lessons in lower elementary or kindergarten age. They might have taken lessons for a couple of years, felt like they didn't make much progress, and then got interrupted due to a move or scheduling conflicts. Life is busy, so I understand the concern that if you go back to music, it might be a long-term commitment that's hard to keep up and might not lead to completed goals.

I think there's a lot to consider. Firstly, music really is a long journey. It's different from things I would consider "hobbies" for people, which could include art class, archery, or soccer (some people will make these primary disciplines and participate in them for life, my point here is just to point out that music also plays a role in overall brain development, not just in playing music for fun). There are many developmental aspects happening when studying music—it's not just about the experience of performing a song. Musical skills are part of overall creative development and brain development in general. It affects fine motor skills, long-term planning, and listening skills, among other things. It's quite different from other activities kids engage in.

Another point is that not all music teachers are the same. There are so many different skill levels and approaches to teaching. Some parents feel their child didn't achieve much in a couple of years, which might be due to the teaching approach or the match between teacher and student. If a child has a strong learning style preference—whether visual, auditory, or kinesthetic—it's important to find a teacher whose approach matches. Past experiences may not be indicative of future success because there are so many variables, including the skill level of the teacher and the timing for the student. Sometimes, starting at a slightly older age makes a big difference.

Past experiences don't have to define the future. Just because music lessons didn't fully click the first time doesn't mean they won't now. Children grow, develop new interests, and reach stages where they're more ready to engage deeply with music. Likewise, the right teacher and approach can reignite enthusiasm and open new doors.

So, if you're feeling hesitant, I encourage you not to give up. The long-term benefits of music are profound and far-reaching, and sometimes a fresh start with the right changes can lead to truly rewarding progress.

Parent: How do music lessons fit into the big picture for child development? I've heard things about how they help academically or socially, but are these benefits really significant?

Mr. Michael: Music lessons are far more than just a fun, recreational activity. They play a significant role in a child's overall development, fostering skills and abilities that extend well beyond the music itself. In fact, many developmental benefits that music naturally provides were once more prevalent in everyday life but have diminished with the rise of digital activities.

For example, past generations often experienced music through folk songs sung by family members or interactive, song-based games on the playground. These activities helped develop a child's sense of steady beat through physical movement, such as bouncing to music as an infant or participating in clapping games. Today's digital environments, while engaging, often lack these physical, rhythm-based interactions, which can impact the development of motor coordination and reflex organization.

Music lessons reintroduce and strengthen these foundational skills. Identifying and moving to a steady beat helps children with body coordination and synchronization, both independently and in group settings. Similarly, the ability to hear and accurately echo sounds is crucial for language development, phonics, and reading skills. While some children naturally excel in these areas, music education ensures that all children have the opportunity to develop them.

Beyond these basics, music fosters critical life skills. It nurtures creativity, teaching children how to think innovatively and express themselves uniquely. Music also enhances organizational abilities and goal setting. Learning a song or mastering an instrument involves breaking down complex tasks into manageable steps—a skill that is transferable to any area of life.

Furthermore, playing music with others promotes social and emotional growth. It fosters empathy, openness, and a sense of community, helping bridge divides between individuals from different backgrounds. Music places everyone on equal footing, encouraging collaboration and mutual respect.

Creativity, cultivated through music, is not just an artistic skill; it's an essential life skill. It empowers individuals to approach problems without clear solutions confidently. creative thinking supports mental health, self-expression, and resilience. Music helps raise well-rounded students who are equipped with the tools to manage stress, connect with others, and face challenges with confidence.

In essence, music lessons are a vital developmental block in raising healthy, capable, and creative individuals prepared for the complexities of life.

Parent: I worry about adding more to our schedule, especially since my kids already struggle a bit with homework and keeping up with their activities. How much time do they realistically need to devote to practicing, and what happens if they can't fit it in every day?

Mr. Michael: One of the most common concerns I hear from parents is, "We're just too busy for music lessons." I completely understand—life today is incredibly demanding with work, school, extracurricular activities, and family commitments. There's no magic solution that adds more hours to the day. However, it's important to shift the perspective from viewing it as just another extracurricular activity to recognizing it as an essential part of a child's education.

Consider this: you likely wouldn't say, "We're too busy for math right now because of soccer practice, Taekwondo, and work." That's because math is viewed as an educational priority. Music, while different from core academic subjects, also plays a significant role in cognitive development, discipline, creativity, and emotional well-being. The first step is deciding whether music is a luxury or a valuable, integral part of your child's growth.

That said, I know this isn't just about priorities—it's about logistics. If in-person lessons feel overwhelming due to scheduling, consider alternatives. Online lessons with a live teacher, app-based instruction, or even video tutorials can be effective, especially during particularly busy seasons. It's similar to how a math tutor might offer the most personalized support, but if that's not feasible, practicing with Khan Academy or math workbooks is still beneficial. The key is continuity, even if the format shifts temporarily.

When it comes to daily practice, many families struggle with it becoming just another chore. Open, honest communication with your child's music teacher can make a big difference. As a teacher, I've had students who were attentive during lessons but told their parents they found certain songs boring. When parents shared this feedback, I could adjust the material to better engage the student. There's an abundance of music available, and if one piece isn't resonating, there are countless others to explore.

Another common challenge is that students often don't know how to break their assignments into manageable steps. Some teachers naturally provide detailed guidance, but if not, don't hesitate to ask for help. Request specific instructions, like practicing one line at a time or focusing on one hand at a time. Clear, small goals make practice sessions more productive and less frustrating.

Consistency is key, but it doesn't have to be rigid. Aim for short, focused practice sessions at the same time each day, such as before or after dinner. It's more effective (and enjoyable) for a child to have 10 positive minutes of practice daily than to cram an hour once a week. The goal is quality over quantity: sitting down with a specific, achievable task in mind and ending with a sense of accomplishment.

For busy parents, remember that music lessons don't have to add stress to your schedule. By prioritizing music as an educational tool, being flexible with logistics, and focusing on consistent, goal-oriented practice, you can integrate music into your child's life in a manageable way.

Parent: My oldest didn't enjoy music lessons when we tried it before. They got frustrated and didn't seem to make much progress. How do you handle kids who feel discouraged, or what would you do differently to make lessons more engaging for kids who may not naturally take to music?

Mr. Michael: Discouragement is a natural part of any learning process, and music is no exception. In fact, this is an area where team sports often have an advantage over music lessons. In sports, the sense of accountability to a team can motivate players to push through difficult times. Similarly, music programs that are performance-based can help students stick with their practice because they're working toward a shared goal, like participating in a concert. This structure can be helpful, but it's not the right fit for every student. Not every child is energized by the idea of performing in a group, and sometimes, a strict performance focus can limit opportunities for personal creativity and exploration.

In life, many meaningful projects are deeply personal, requiring internal motivation rather than external accountability. Developing the resilience to overcome discouragement without relying on a team dynamic is a valuable skill in itself. When I work with a student who hits a plateau or feels burned out, the first step is to identify the root cause of their discouragement.

For older students, especially those juggling heavy academic loads with activities like AP classes, it can be frustrating to attend lessons feeling unprepared. In these cases, patience is key. Life goes through busy seasons, and it's important to normalize this reality. As adults, we experience it too—whether it's pausing a hobby due to work demands or new family responsibilities. The goal isn't perfection; it's persistence. Even if a student can't practice much during a hectic season, maintaining the habit of attending lessons keeps the door open for growth when their schedule allows.

Adjusting expectations without giving up entirely is a crucial skill. I applaud parents who keep their children enrolled in lessons even during busy times. Teachers also play a vital role in this process. We should avoid shaming students for limited practice and instead find ways to keep them engaged. For example, if a student is overwhelmed, I might shift from structured classical pieces to improvisation, learning a pop song by ear, or exploring simpler music that keeps their creative muscles active. It's like going for a walk when you don't have time for a full workout—it keeps the habit alive.

Another common source of discouragement is a lack of connection to the music itself. While I teach classical piano and believe in its value, not every student feels inspired by traditional repertoire. If a student isn't connecting with the material, it's important to adjust. There's a vast world of music to explore

The teacher-student relationship also significantly impacts a student's experience. Not every student will click with every teacher, and that's okay. If a student seems disengaged, it might be worth exploring whether a different teaching style or personality would be a better fit. Larger music schools often make this easier, offering a variety of instructors under one roof. However, even with individual teachers, meeting and evaluating different options can help find the right connection.

Teachers must also reflect on their own approach. Encouragement is essential. I learned this lesson firsthand. My first formal lessons were on the trumpet in fourth grade, and I eventually quit—not because I disliked the trumpet, but because the teacher was grumpy, unmotivating, and made the experience unenjoyable. That shaped me as a teacher, reminding me of the importance of being a positive, supportive presence. Students thrive when they feel encouraged and valued.

Ultimately, overcoming discouragement in music requires a combination of patience, flexibility, and support. It's about helping students adjust their expectations, stay connected to their love of music, and know that setbacks are just part of the journey—not the end of it.

Parent: Music lessons aren't cheap, and we're a middle-class family with a lot of expenses. Are the benefits of lessons really worth the cost, or are there alternative ways to expose kids to music without the same level of commitment?

Mr. Michael: Music lessons undeniably come at a cost, and while I can't speak to how public education systems should ideally handle music education, I do believe that in a perfect world, students would receive comprehensive, ongoing music instruction. This would include both general music appreciation and the development of specific skills tied to mastering an instrument, such as the violin, guitar, or piano. In reality, however, many students receive their only formal music education through private lessons, which means these lessons often need to serve as an all-in-one solution.

One of the aspects I find most challenging about music education is how easily it can become elitist. Students whose families can invest more in their education often have a clear advantage. I genuinely wish there was a simple solution to this disparity. Despite this, when faced with the question of whether the cost of music lessons is worth it, my answer is a resounding yes.

The cost of music lessons reflects the value of having a qualified, dedicated teacher guiding your child's development. This investment supports:

- Well-developed listening skills

- Refined fine motor skills

- Cognitive connections between the eyes, ears, and hands, functioning in real-time

- Synchronized collaboration skills for playing with others

- Exposure to a broad range of musical styles and artistic experiences

And the list goes on.

When it comes to supporting our children's growth, we all have three key resources to draw from: **time, money, and expertise.** If financial resources are limited, parents can invest time and effort, working directly with their child on musical activities. Thanks to the wealth of information available online, it's entirely possible to educate yourself on best practices in music instruction for children—if you have the time and energy to do so.

However, we all face limitations in these areas. Balancing time, financial resources, and personal knowledge is a challenge for every family. As a music teacher with over 25 years of experience, I've dedicated a significant portion of my life to developing my skills and understanding of how best to nurture musical growth in students. This depth of knowledge is part of what makes the investment in music lessons worthwhile.

Ultimately, music lessons are more than just an extracurricular activity—they are an investment in your child's cognitive, emotional, and creative development. The skills gained through music education extend far beyond the practice room, enriching every area of a child's life.

Parent: I'm not musically inclined myself, so I wouldn't know how to help my kids with practice or even gauge their progress. Is that a problem? How involved do parents need to be for their kids to succeed?

Mr. Michael: I often encounter parents who feel they can't be actively involved in their child's music lessons because they themselves had little or no formal music education. While I understand and sympathize with this concern, I don't believe it's as significant a hindrance as many parents assume. In fact, the most important thing students need to be successful isn't specialized knowledge—it's encouragement.

Learning to play a musical instrument takes time, effort, and perseverance. Students need to be reminded, praised, and recognized for the hard work they put in. This doesn't require any musical expertise. Simply being present to listen, showing genuine interest, and cheering your child on can make a tremendous difference in their motivation and confidence.

Parents without musical backgrounds might need a teacher's guidance to understand the smaller tasks that make up "practicing", but once a plan is in place, any attentive adult can help. You can support your child by helping them stick to their practice plan, reminding them of small tasks to complete, and ensuring they're not just sent off to practice alone without direction. It's not about supervising every minute but offering structure and accountability.

Open communication between parents, students, and teachers is invaluable. This doesn't mean becoming a helicopter parent or intervening at every minor frustration, but it does mean being an active participant in your child's learning journey. Teachers only see students for a small fraction of their week, and parents often have insights that can help make lessons more effective.

For example, if your child frequently comes home saying they don't understand an assignment, they may have been too shy to ask questions during the lesson. Sharing this with the teacher can help address gaps in understanding. If your child isn't inspired by certain pieces and you know of music they love, passing that information along can guide the teacher in selecting more engaging material. Even general updates about how your child is doing in school can provide helpful context for understanding their learning style, strengths, and areas where they might need extra support.

Finally, don't underestimate your own potential to be involved. I've worked with many parents and grandparents who decided to learn an instrument alongside their child. Families that play music together often have some of the most rewarding and enjoyable experiences. Not only does this create a unique bonding opportunity, but it also fosters a shared understanding of the learning process.

So, if you're feeling hesitant, remember that your involvement doesn't require formal music training. Encouragement, goal-setting support, open communication, and even learning alongside your child can have a lasting, positive impact on their musical journey.

Parent: My kids already have extracurriculars they enjoy, like sports and scouts. Is there a strong reason to prioritize music lessons over these other activities, or would it make sense to stick with what they're already doing?

Mr. Michael: Kids today are undeniably busier than ever. Between physical activities, social commitments, academic responsibilities, and creative pursuits like music, there's a lot to juggle—and the truth is, no one can do it all. I don't believe that every child needs to take formal music lessons or learn to play an instrument throughout their entire childhood. However, I do believe that every child should be engaged with music in some capacity.

It's up to parents to explore different opportunities, both at home and in the community, to provide musical exposure. This can include listening to a wide variety of music, singing together, attending live performances, or giving children the chance to try an instrument. They may or may not develop a lasting passion for it, but first-hand experiences are invaluable for discovering what resonates with them.

When students start lessons with me, my basic goal is to make it through the first 18 months together. The first 6 to 12 months are foundational—there's so much basic ground to cover that students often don't have an accurate sense of whether they truly enjoy playing an instrument until they've moved beyond that initial learning curve. In those early months, lessons can feel more like work as students build fundamental skills.

Taking piano lessons for just three months doesn't provide enough time to form a well-rounded opinion about the experience. However, after two years of lessons, students (and parents) can make a much more informed judgment about their interest and connection to the instrument. If a student decides to stop formal music lessons, I still encourage them to find ways to stay musically engaged. Music does require you to become a performer to be meaningful.

If a child discovers their true passion lies in gymnastics, engineering, or another field, that's perfectly okay. The knowledge and skills gained through music can enhance other areas of life, like problem-solving in engineering or serving as a creative outlet for mental health. Even if they don't continue playing an instrument, students with hands-on musical experience often develop a deeper appreciation for the arts that stays with them for life.

Ultimately, music can be a lifelong companion, whether as a hobby, a career, or simply as a source of joy and connection. The goal is to create positive, lasting experiences with music, however it fits into a child's life.

Parent: I know you're a music teacher, but you're also a parent. Have you had your own children take music lessons, and if so, what was your experience? Did you face any challenges, and how did you handle them?

Mr. Michael: People often assume that because I'm a music teacher, my three children all started taking piano lessons in preschool. The reality, however, is very different.

First of all, I've never been the primary music teacher for any of my kids. While I'm deeply engaged with them musically and can support them when needed, I believe in giving them the opportunity to experience the student-teacher dynamic with other musicians. Just as I've taught piano to the children of close friends, I wanted my own children to have that objective learning relationship, free from the complexities that come with being both parent and teacher.

One of my children is a particularly talented singer, a gift she likely inherited from her mother. While she's had some formal instruction, we've focused more on performance-based experiences, especially in musical theater, where she has the chance to sing both solo and as part of an ensemble. As a preteen, she independently taught herself to play both the ukulele and piano. Perhaps because music is my profession, she felt more comfortable learning on her own, outside of what she might perceive as the "watchful eyes" of others. She was so determined one weekend to master the ukulele that she spent hours hunched over, leading us to a doctor visit the following week due to neck strain (thankfully, she recovered quickly). We've always kept instruments readily accessible at home, which has allowed her to explore music freely. Since she loves performing, we continue to create opportunities for her to grow and shine on stage.

My other two children are the opposite—they're almost "allergic" to the stage and have never performed publicly. One of them plays the drums and enjoys his weekly lessons. He has a drum kit in his room but rarely practices. Despite this, he has a strong connection with his teacher, which keeps him engaged, and he's progressed quickly thanks to his natural talent. He has no ambitions to pursue music more seriously, and that's perfectly fine. He also has learning disabilities, and the cross-body coordination required for drumming, along with processing complex rhythms, has been incredibly beneficial for his brain development. The positive relationship with his teacher, who shares his sense of humor, has made music an enjoyable and meaningful part of his life.

My third child decided at age 12 to channel her intense focus into playing the guitar. Despite having ADHD, she spends hours practicing outside of her weekly lessons. She often selects her own projects, developing a unique musical taste that her teacher both supports and expands by introducing her to new styles. Their lessons are highly collaborative, with her teacher adapting to her interests while ensuring she builds strong foundational skills. Music has become a core part of her identity, helping her manage her mental health and providing a creative outlet that she thrives in.

Perhaps my guitar-playing daughter will become a music teacher one day, as she loves helping others and has a genuine passion for music. But regardless of the paths my children choose, their journeys have been uniquely their own. By paying attention to their individual needs and interests, we've helped them find personal connections to music, fostering positive, enriching experiences that are as diverse as they are.

Parent: What's your approach for helping kids discover whether they truly enjoy music? I don't want to force my kids into something that will feel like a chore.

Mr. Michael: When it comes to discussing "musical" versus "non-musical" children, I want to be very clear: I don't believe there is such a thing as a non-musical child. This is a core belief I hold, and it shapes how I approach teaching. Many adults feel they aren't musical, but this perception often stems from being told at some point that they lack musical talent. Yet, I can't think of a single adult I know who actively dislikes music. This suggests that our relationship with music is deeply influenced by childhood experiences. As parents and teachers, we hold incredible power to shape a child's narrative, fostering the belief that they are not only creative but inherently musical. We can empower them to engage with music actively, rather than just passively consuming it.

The question isn't whether a child likes music—it's how they like to engage with it. One of the most basic aspects of this is genre preference. Musical tastes are often influenced by family experiences. While a parent's love for country music doesn't guarantee their child will feel the same, family musical traditions do create connections. It's wise to build on these connections, allowing children to explore songs and styles they enjoy as part of their musical journey.

That said, I don't believe we should only teach children the songs they already like. This would be akin to asking a four-year-old what they want to eat for every meal and always serving that. We encourage children to try a variety of foods to develop a balanced diet, just as we should expose them to diverse musical experiences. Over time, they may develop preferences, which is natural and healthy. For example, my own kids find it amusing that I'll eat almost anything, but I'm not particularly fond of carrots. They've seen me eat carrots occasionally, though, to show that preferences aren't rigid judgments about what's "good" or "bad"—they're simply personal tastes.

Similarly, when assessing a child's musical interests, we need to be open to a variety of entry points. This includes embracing modern digital music pathways. If a student wants to study DJing or beat production instead of traditional piano lessons—or alongside them—that's perfectly valid. Music is a vast landscape, and every path within it holds value.

Lastly, we must recognize and respect different learning styles. A student who plays well by ear is not inherently more musical than one who relies on reading sheet music. I didn't play well by earHowever, none of my children read music well or use it on a regular basis when they play. If a particular teaching method isn't working with a student, it's important to adapt and explore different approaches rather than concluding the student isn't musical. Every child has the potential to enjoy and engage with music; it's up to us to help them find the pathway that feels right for them.

Parent: Are there certain signs that would suggest music lessons might not be the best fit for my kids, at least right now? I want to make sure we're not setting them up for unnecessary stress.

Mr. Michael: Deciding when to stop music lessons can be a challenging decision for both parents and students. For young learners, it's important to consider developmental readiness. If a child lacks the fine motor skills, working memory, or reading ability needed for instruments like the piano or violin, it might be better to shift focus to a more general music class. These classes can help them develop foundational skills such as moving to a beat, singing age-appropriate songs in tune, and building confidence in their solo singing voice.

As I've mentioned before, I typically recommend that students continue lessons for at least a year, ideally reaching the 18-month mark before making a final decision about quitting. This allows them to move past the initial hurdles of learning new physical skills and concepts, giving them a chance to experience the true joy of making music once they've gained some proficiency.

Musical development generally occurs in two key phases. For children around the age of seven and younger, the focus should be on absorbing musical language—much like how young children learn to speak before they read or write. During this phase, it's more about input (listening, feeling rhythm, singing) rather than output (performance skills). After about age eight, children begin applying these foundational skills more actively.

If a student is struggling during this early phase, it's important to explore different learning styles before considering quitting. This might involve:

- Trying varied learning methods: Combining visual learning (like reading music) with auditory learning (memorizing or playing by ear).

- Exploring different genres: Introducing a wider range of musical styles to find what they connect with.

- Switching instruments: Sometimes, the issue isn't a lack of interest in music itself but a disconnect with the chosen instrument. A child who doesn't enjoy piano might thrive with the guitar, drums, or another instrument.

If none of these approaches work, it doesn't mean the child isn't creative or musical. It may simply not be the right time for structured weekly lessons. In such cases, I often recommend revisiting the idea of lessons between the ages of eight and twelve, when cognitive and motor skills have further developed.

For example, I didn't start formal piano lessons until I was 11, simply because we didn't have a piano at home earlier and the financial opportunity wasn't available. Yet, within six years, I was majoring in music in college and even started teaching. This shows that it's never too late to start learning an instrument.

Lastly, remember that formal music lessons are not the only way to be musical. If lessons aren't the right fit, there are countless other ways to engage with music—whether through singing, listening, composing, participating in school music programs, or exploring digital music production. The key is to keep the love of music alive, in whatever form feels right for the individual.

Key Takeaways

- Music lessons build lifelong skills – Beyond playing an instrument, music develops discipline, creativity, and problem-solving.

- Past struggles don't mean future failure – The right teacher, timing, or instrument can change a child's experience.

- Parental support matters most – Encouragement and consistency are more important than musical expertise.

- Music and academics complement each other – Learning music enhances focus, time management, and resilience.

After all the questions, the doubts, and the practical concerns, one truth remains: music is worth it. Every musical journey is different. But the bigger picture is clear: music is more than just an extracurricular activity. It's a tool for connection, for growth, for understanding the world in a richer way.

EPILOGUE

Writing this book has been a challenge to myself to go through "The Process" as Seth Godin calls it, and to put my work out there, perfect or not. I sincerely hope to make a second edition someday, as I already see opportunities to improve on this book–so I welcome your feedback and discussion on what you have read here.

We have set up a page of tools and resources on our website at www.newsongsmusic.com/manual for you as well.

If you have read this far and are not already a "Music Maker"- the way I refer to all of our students and their families at NewSongs- I would love to thank you and offer you a few gifts.

If you are in our local area (Sacramento, CA) I can offer you a trial lesson at our school for a reduced rate. Just email my team and I at welcome@newsongsmusic.com and we will get that set up for you. You can also just tour the school and meet with one of our directors for free at any time. Booking links for a visit are also available at www.newsongsmusic.com/manual

If you want to keep in touch with the rest of the things we are doing with music education, feel free to follow us:

Facebook: @Newsongsmusic

Instagram: @newsongsmusic

LinkedIn: www.linkedin.com/company/newsongs-music/

Lastly, I am happy to hear from you directly with your thoughts and comments, success stories and questions. You can reach me at michael@newsongsmusic.com.

Thank you again for being a part of this creative adventure with me.

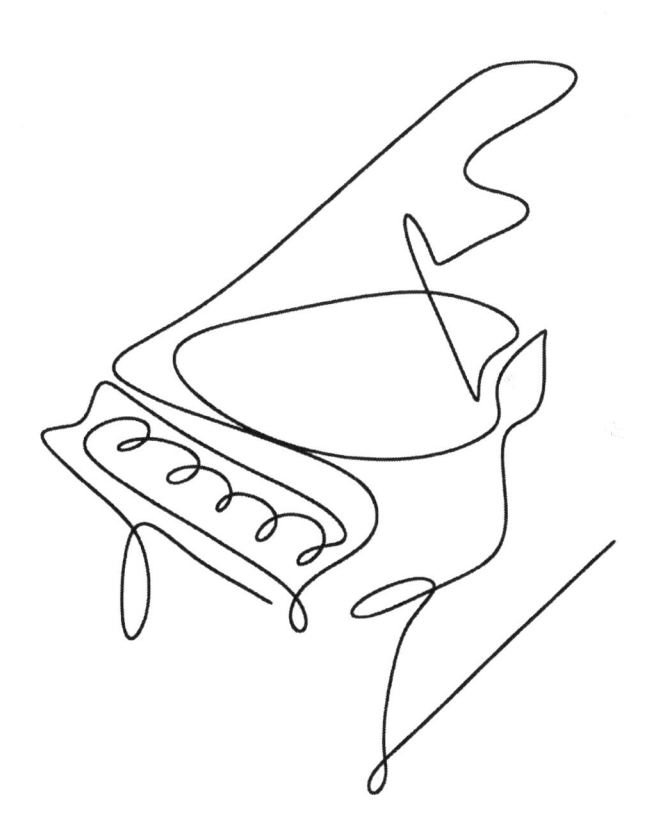

ABOUT THE AUTHOR

Michael Hemsworth is a lifelong music educator and passionate advocate for creative learning. Graduating from the University of California, Davis with a degree in music at just 18, he quickly launched a life of purpose—marrying his wife of over 20 years, becoming a father, and founding NewSongs School of Music all within a year. With over 25 years of experience in music education, Michael began teaching piano lessons at 16 and has since dedicated his career to inspiring students of all ages. Today, he leads a thriving educational community across four NewSongs locations, serving more than 1,300 students weekly. Whether in a classroom, library, or private lesson, he brings energy, warmth, and a ukulele to every session. When he's not sharing music, Michael enjoys time with his family, traveling, and hosting joyful celebrations for every occasion imaginable.

Made in the USA
Columbia, SC
05 April 2025